201 BEST QUESTIONS TO ASK ON YOUR INTERVIEW

201 BEST QUESTIONS TO ASK ON YOUR INTERVIEW

JOHN KADOR

McGRAW-HILL

NEW YORK   CHICAGO SAN FRANCISCO   LISBON   LONDON
MADRID   MEXICO CITY   MILAN   NEW DELHI   SAN JUAN
SEOUL   SINGAPORE   SYDNEY   TORONTO

McGraw-Hill

A Division of The McGraw·Hill Companies

9 0   DOC/DOC   0 9 8 7 6 5

ISBN 0-07-138773-0

This book was set in New Times Roman by MM Design 2000, Inc.

Printed and bound by R. R. Donnelley & Sons Company.

This book is printed on recycled, acid-free paper containing a minimum of 50% recycled, de-inked fiber

To my father,
for modeling so well the responsibilities
and contentments of self-employment.

To my mother,
for teaching me the reasons why
self precedes *employment*.

And to my entire family
for reminding me that work is play
with a larger social purpose.

CONTENTS

CONTENTS

FOREWORD

A blank sheet. A clean slate. A fresh start.

There are various ways to describe the challenge any author faces when first sitting down to write a book. So much promise and potential on one hand, so much raw material that cries out for order on the other.

The same opportunity confronts every job applicant I've met in more than 20 years of counseling and nurturing prospective employees. The seed exists in every book, in every job interview, in every human encounter, to shape and control: to write the story you choose, to obtain the outcome you seek, to speak the truth into existence. Against this backdrop, John Kador has created an empowering book for all those committed to advancing their careers.

If we in the human resources field can offer job seekers one thing, it is that sense of empowerment. Empowerment is the engine that gets it done. Empowerment is different from confidence, because it is more than an attitude or a state of mind—it's a state of being.

Empowerment isn't giving the villager a fish to eat; it's teaching him or her how to fish. Empowerment is a corollary to education. Just as education provides the framework for advancement—not simply in mastering a body of knowledge, but in knowing how to acquire more—so a sense of empowerment enables job hunters to take control and craft a career. In doing so, what matters isn't just the current job, but the path taken—the relationship to work *throughout life*. And as John demonstrates so compellingly in this book, empowerment begins with the questions applicants ask.

So much creativity and insight has gone into the concept of the "informational interview," thanks largely to Richard Bolles and his marvelous classic, *What Color Is Your Parachute?* For job seekers, the informational interview at once reduces stress, manages expectations, and elicits—what else?—information. For the employer, the informational interview is just as useful.

But John has gone the process one better. In showing job seekers how to interview interviewers, he has taken the informational interview to the next level. As this practice takes hold, the benefits to employees and employers alike will be palpable.

How do I know this? Because empowerment doesn't happen as some sort of grand revelation; it's in the details, the small etchings on the clean slate, the right questions asked in the right way, at the right time. And because, for me, this process really worked—though I couldn't have described it as such at the time.

I was born and went to school in the small community of Tarboro, North Carolina. I recognized in John's book a road map of my own early experiences. As a young girl, I saw how people's lives were shaped by their career opportunities, and I sensed that my own advancement was keyed to the kind of inquisitor I was. As a student in Project Upward Bound, a program for academically achieving, college-bound, disadvantaged students, I left North Carolina to expand my education, eventually working at the National Academy of Sciences in Washington, D.C.

Throughout my journey, one common thread emerged: The quality of the answers I received was related directly to the pointed nature of the questions I asked. The more engaged I was, the more those around me responded. This process was nonverbal as well as verbal. Without articulating it even to myself, I was advancing my credentials by being proactive and perhaps, now and again, a bit provocative.

Today, having founded a company in the business of helping people transform jobs into meaningful careers (and, yes, become empowered), I can say without reservation that even in an unsettled economy, talent will out. Good people, by definition, take charge. The interview is your fresh start.

We can thank John Kador that it will never again be a blank sheet.

JANICE BRYANT HOWROYD
Founder, CEO, Chairman, ACT-1 Personnel Services
Torrance, California

ACKNOWLEDGMENTS

Professionals in the staffing industry may be among the hardest-working people in the world. I am gratified to be able to acknowledge so many excellent people who carved time out of their busy days to help me with this book.

To these authorities, staffing professionals all, I express my gratitude: Anna Braasch, Kimberly Bedore, Janice Brookshier, Kate Brothers, Robert Conlin, Bryan Debenport, Mariette Durack Edwards, Sandra Grabczynski, Jeanette Grill, Scott Hagen, Joel Hamroff, Charles Handler, Beau Harris, Bob Johnson, Kathi Jones, Robin M. Johnson, Richard Kathnelson, Wayne Kale, Houston Landry, Grant Lehman, Joeseph LePla, Nancy Levine, Sonja C. Parker, Liz Reiersen, Jason Rodd, Tony Stanic, Susan Trainer, Tom Thrower, and Robin Upton. On occasion, I chose to ignore their advice and suggestions. If there are errors in this book, therefore, they are all mine.

Special thanks go to Janice Bryant Howroyd for writing a very personal Foreword and to Melanie Allred Mays and Gary Ames for giving my readers the benefit of some sharp intellectual property. Part III of this book would be impoverished, indeed, without their contributions. I thank Melanie Mays for the Company Cultural Survey and Gary Ames and Dr. Wendell Williams for the organization and many of the questions in Chapters 9–12.

Once again I am indebted to Dr. John Sullivan, professor and head of Human Resource Management at San Francisco State University, for sharing with me his experience and perspective on every aspect of the staffing process. I especially appreciate John for sharing the "superstar" questions in Chapter 13.

For reading the manuscript and giving me many valuable suggestions, I appreciate Anna Beth Payne, associate director of the Counseling and Student Development Center, Northern Illinois University, and Alan Farber, assistant director, Career Planning and Placement Center, Northern Illinois University, DeKalb, Illinois.

And finally, I'd like to thank the many job seekers on job boards around the world who contacted me after reading my increasingly desperate posts for great and dumb interview questions. Your emails make an author's day.

Note to readers: Many of the staffing professionals who helped me with the book are willing to be resources for readers. Check my Web site (www.jkador.com) for a list of their contact information.

INTRODUCTION

The landscape for job seekers today is more treacherous than at any time in recent memory. In other words, if you want a job today, you may actually have to work for it.

Just a few months ago, the job interview was an opportunity for candidates to present their demands and screen the best offers. Today the tide has turned and employers are running the show again. It's no longer enough to be qualified. If you want a job in today's business environment, you have to shine in the job interview.

One way to really shine is by asking questions. Questions are the best way for you to demonstrate that you understand the company's challenges, emphasize how you can help the company meet them, and show your interest in the most unmistakable manner possible— by actually asking for the position. This book will help arm you with new interview questions and techniques for selling yourself and getting the job you want.

After more than a decade of job seekers calling the shots, the collapse of the dot-com economy has resulted in a much more restricted hiring environment. Employers can now afford to be much more choosy. With dozens or even hundreds of applicants competing for every job, employers are raising their standards.

Competition for jobs has never been higher. The ease of recruiting with the Internet has radically decreased the expense of accumulating résumés. Today, you are competing not only with other job seekers from the same community, but with highly qualified people from all over the world. Scared and frustrated, employees still fortunate to have a job are staying put, decreasing opportunities for career advancement.

For organizations, the stakes for making the right hiring decision are higher than ever before. Business moves more quickly today than ever before. Organizations are leaner and more networked. If a critical task is not performed, the whole operation is at risk of falling apart. Often a critical hire is all that stands between organizational failure and success. Organizations today have no guarantee of second chances. They must get it right the first time.

RAISING THE ANTE FOR JOB SEEKERS

In their struggle to survive, increasingly lean organizations are making decisions that also raise the ante for job seekers. Companies today are putting a premium on human productivity. They want to hire people who can add significant value from day one. Any job candidate who cannot demonstrate his or her value proposition within a few minutes into the job interview cannot be expected to advance.

Few organizations today are content to hire merely qualified performers capable of acceptable performance. In a buyer's market, they feel they don't have to settle for anything less than superstars at every level of the company. These organizations look for individuals who can demonstrate consistently outstanding results as well as the ability to stretch well beyond traditional measures of performance. These are the movers and change agents who can apply thought leadership to the challenges of the organization.

Interviewers today want to see immediate evidence that you are action-oriented, engaged with the long term, committed, zestful, and curious. These are the attributes that will get you a job. If you act passive, disengaged, short term–driven, self-centered, and apathetic, you'll be passed over. Your ability to ask meaningful questions will tell the interviewer if you project the first set of attributes or the latter.

Does the contemporary job interview seem like a high hurdle to jump? It is. And you won't get more than a few minutes to demonstrate that you are a world-class contributor.

Organizations have beefed up the entire employee selection process to weed out the amateurs, impostors, and other wanna-bes. The job interview has received more than its share of attention as a critical vehicle to achieve organizational goals. If you have been interviewing, you know that employers have developed dramatically more sophisticated interviewing and selection techniques. You see evidence of these developments in every aspect of the selection process, from the job interview to exhaustive background checks and drug testing. This book gives you a shot at understanding what you will be up against in the new world of job interviews.

Many job hunters think their primary goal is to get to the job interview. Wrong! If you think the primary goal of the job hunter is to get a job offer, you are getting warmer, but you are still a day late and dollar short. In reality, the primary goal of the job hunter is to get an offer for a job that is a good fit with his or her short- and long-term requirements—in other words, a position that is sustainable for both the job hunter and the employer.

To succeed at this part of the job hunt requires the job seeker to interview the interviewer. By this point in the process, the chemistry between the employer and job seeker should be pretty good. If there are any remaining candidates, their abilities should be fairly similar, so you are now competing on softer issues. If you are still in the running, chances are the employer wants to hire you at least as much as you want to be hired. Now the tables are turned, and it is your opportunity to determine if this is the job that's best for your career. Now you get to interview the interviewer, and in doing so you have another opportunity to reinforce your desirability as the best candidate for the job. This book shows you how.

To ground the book in reality, I've asked hundreds of recruiters, job coaches, and hiring managers for the most memorably good and bad questions they have heard from job candidates. Some of these questions are brilliant in their insight, depth, and elegance. Others are just as effective in terminating the interview with extreme prejudice. Whether the questions are memorably good or memorably bad, learn from the former and avoid the latter. The best of these memorable questions, with comments from the recruiters, are peppered throughout the book and are separately indexed in the back.

AN INTERVIEW BETWEEN
THE READER AND THE AUTHOR

AUTHOR: Thank you for opening the book. Did you have any trouble finding it?

READER: No, the directions you gave me were great. The book was right there in the Career Section, just where you said it would be.

AUTHOR: That's great. Well, I appreciate your interest in my book. Please make yourself comfortable. Can I get you a cup of coffee?

READER: Thank you, no. Maybe later.

AUTHOR: As you know, we will be talking to you about buying this book. This book gives you a powerful approach to job interviewing by teaching you to ask questions that put the candidate in the best light possible. By asking the right questions you can quickly demonstrate the unique value proposition you alone offer and highlight why you can immediately ease the business pain of the company you are interviewing with.

READER: A problem-solution approach. Sounds promising. Do you mind if I take notes?

AUTHOR: Not at all. Now, we hope to use this exchange to get to know each other better. Maybe you can start by telling me about how you expect this book to advance your career objectives.

READER: In my job interviews, I want to be ready to ask questions of such intelligence and elegance that they knock the interviewer's socks off and immediately set me apart as a force to be reckoned with.

AUTHOR: I like the way you put that.

READER: I want my questions to reinforce the reality that I am conspicuously the best person for the job and then to ask for the job in a way that the interviewer will want to endorse my application and recommend making me the strongest offer possible.

AUTHOR: This book will certainly help you do that. At this point, allow me to describe the book to you in terms of its content and how I structured it to help you make an immediately favorable impression at job interviews. In this way, you will have the information you need to make a determination about whether purchasing this book will advance your career objectives. Our book-buying philosophy here at McGraw-Hill is that either a book-buying decision is a good two-way fit, or it's not a fit at all. How does that sound?

READER: It sounds great. May I ask a question?

AUTHOR: Yes, of course.

READER: You asked me about my requirements. What are *your* requirements?

AUTHOR: My requirements are simple. Do you have $12.95?

READER: Yes.

AUTHOR: You've satisfied my requirements.

READER: $12.95? Is that all? I would have thought a book of this earth-shaking value would cost a lot more.

AUTHOR: I appreciate the flattery, but this book is not about sucking up. Sweet talk is not going to advance your career. Questions framed with intelligence and presented strategically will. So let me give you a quick description of what the book offers. The book has three sections. Part I discusses the rules for asking the best questions. Chapter 1, "Why You Have to Question," reviews why it is imperative to have questions and offers some guidelines for asking questions in the strongest way possible. Chapter 2, "Questions You Should Never Initiate," tells you what subject areas to avoid. Chapters 3, "When to Question," 4, "Do Your Homework," and 5, "Do You Mind If I Take Notes?" deal with the issues of timing, research, and note taking, respectively.

Part II lists most of the 201 best questions promised in the title. These are the questions you will use to form the basis of the questions you ask in your next job interview. Some questions are most appropriate for different types of interview situations. Chapters 6, "Questions for Headhunters, Recruiters, and Staffing Agencies," 7, "Questions for Human Resources," and 8, "Questions for Hiring Managers," list the questions that each of these groups will find particularly meaningful.

I hope you find Part III especially useful. It deals with the most common job interview scenarios and recommends killer questions for each. For example, Chapter 9, "Exploring Questions," looks at questions that demonstrate your interest in the job and the company. Chapter 10, "Defensive Questions," helps protect you from taking the wrong job. Chapter 11, "Feedback Questions," focuses on questions that allow the interviewer to identify objections so you can deal with them. Chapter 12, "Bid-for-Action Questions," suggests phrasings so you can actually ask for the job, an important step that most candidates miss.

READER: I especially appreciate the questions in Chapter 13, "Questions for Superstars." Do candidates really ask such in-your-face questions?

AUTHOR: Some do. It's a question of how confident you are as a candidate. Chapter 14, "You Got an Offer. Congratulations!" deals with the happy outcome that you have received an offer and you want the job. Naturally you have many questions. Chapter 15, "You Blew the Interview. Now What?" looks at the near certainty that at least some of your applications will be rejected. Don't lose heart. There is still hope, if not for another shot at the company, then at least a powerful learning opportunity.

So that's how the book is laid out. Any other questions?

READER: Yes, from what you have just told me, I'm pretty sure that this book is what I need. So can I buy it, read it, and get back to you with any remaining questions?

AUTHOR: Absolutely. Email me at jkador@jkador.com. I welcome your questions, and I wish you the best in your job search.

> JOHN KADOR
> Geneva, Illinois
> January 2002

201 BEST QUESTIONS TO ASK ON YOUR INTERVIEW

THE RULES OF THE GAME

The interviewer's most critical question in a job interview is often the last one.

The interviewer's last question is frequently the most important one. That's when the interviewer smiles and says: "Now, do you have questions for us?" Your response at this point often determines if you continue as a job seeker or transform into a job getter.

There are great questions and dumb questions and, worst of all, no questions at all. This book prepares you for the most neglected part of the job interview: the opportunity for you to ask questions. Part I outlines some rules and principles you can apply in your questioning so that you ask more of the former and fewer of the latter.

But first a quiz.

Of the following five candidate behaviors in the job interview, what behavior do you think recruiters find most unforgivable?

1. Poor personal appearance

2. Overemphasis on money

3. Failure to look at interviewer while interviewing

4. Doesn't ask questions

5. Late to interview

The answer is number 4. Surprised? Candidates who do not ask any questions represent the number one behavior that causes recruiters to lose confidence, according to my admittedly unscientific survey of over 150 recruiters, job coaches, and hiring managers. Still, it's not too bold to make this statement: You cannot succeed in a job interview without asking a number of well-considered questions.

Of course, even great questions will not get you a job offer if you come in with other problems. Here, in order, are the 10 attitude strikeouts that most often condemn job candidates:

1. Doesn't ask questions
2. Condemnation of past employer
3. Inability to take criticism
4. Poor personal appearance
5. Indecisive, cynical, lazy
6. Overbearing, overly aggressive, "know-it-all"
7. Late to interview
8. Failure to look at interviewer while interviewing
9. Unable to express self clearly
10. Overemphasis on money

CHAPTER 1

WHY YOU HAVE TO QUESTION

QUESTIONS ARE NOT AN OPTION

"Now, do you have any questions?"

Every job interview, if the job seeker is lucky, gets to this stage. What you do now controls whether or not you get an offer. The résumé gets you in the door, but whether you leave as a job seeker or an employee depends on how you conduct yourself during the interview.

Some candidates think that when the interviewer says, "Now, do you have any questions?" it's a polite indication that the interview is about over and they are about to wrap up. They couldn't be more mistaken. The question really signals the start of the main course. Everything that came before was just appetizer.

Recruiters are unanimous on this point: Job seekers who fail to ask at least a few intelligent questions are destined to remain job seekers. If you don't ask questions, you leave these impressions:

- You think the job is unimportant or trivial.
- You're uncomfortable asserting yourself.
- You're not intelligent.
- You're easily intimidated.
- You're bored or boring.

Not one of these impressions works in your favor. Of course, not any old questions will do. If you don't think about this in advance, you run the risk of missing a critical opportunity by not asking intelligent questions or by planting your foot in your mouth by asking stupid ones. Good questions show the interviewer that you are interested in the job. Great questions tell the interviewer that you are a force to be reckoned with.

VESTED IN THE INTERVIEW

"I want to know that the candidate in front of me is vested in the job interview," says Janice Bryant Howroyd, founder, CEO, and chairman of Torrance, California–based ACT-1, the largest female, minority-owned employment service in the country. "If the candidate doesn't have any questions, that really clouds my estimation of their interest and ability to engage."

In fact, Bryant Howroyd's practice is to ask just one question, and then immediately throw the ball to the job seeker. Bryant Howroyd's first question, after greeting the job seeker, is:

What is your understanding of our meeting today?

How's that for turning the interview topsy-turvy?

But Bryant Howroyd understands she can tell more from candidates by the quality of their questions than by the quality of their answers. So the next instruction is:

I would now like you to ask me seven questions.

Depending on the quality of the applicant's response to the first query, Bryant Howroyd invites the applicant to ask her from three to seven specific questions. The higher her initial estimation of the applicant, the more questions she requests. What's more, Bryant Howroyd gives the applicant permission to ask her any questions at all. No limits. And then she listens. "I learn a lot more about people by allowing them to ask me what they want to know than by having them tell me what they think I want to know," she says. True, the hiring company ultimately selects the applicant, but "the applicants I most admire insist on being full partners in the selection process," she says.

4

Now, are you really ready for an interview with Janice Bryant Howroyd?

Robin Upton is a career coach at Bernard Haldane Associates, the largest career management firm in the United States. Based in the firm's office in Dallas, Texas, Upton coaches her candidates to ask two questions of the hiring manager. The first question is:

Now that we have talked about my qualifications, do you have any concerns about me fulfilling the responsibilities of this position?

Does it seem counterintuitive to ask the interviewer to articulate his or her concerns? Many candidates think so. But they are being short-sighted, Upton argues. Once objections are stated, the candidate can usually address them in a way that is satisfactory. Unstated objections will doom the candidate every time.

Upton's second question is:

As my direct report in this position, what are the three top priorities you would first like to see accomplished?

This question, she says, effectively determines the hot buttons of the hiring manager, demonstrates the candidate's understanding that every hiring manager has priorities, and underscores the candidate's commitment to action by the final word in the question. Remember, "accomplish" is a term dear to the heart of every hiring manager.

If you don't ask questions in the interview, many recruiters will wonder if you will avoid asking questions on the job. "If I set up a scenario for a technical candidate, and they don't ask qualifying questions, I really wonder if that is how they would approach an application development project," says Kathi Jones, director of Employee Central at Aventail, a Seattle-based provider of extranet services. "Are they letting ego get in the way of asking the hard questions? Do they play on a team or play against the team? I think you can learn as much from someone's questions and their thought process as you can from the answers," she adds.

Here's another wrinkle. Recruiters expect candidates to ask enough questions to form an opinion about whether they want the job or not. If you don't ask enough questions, recruiters who may otherwise be willing to make you an offer may nevertheless reject you because they have no confidence you know what you would be getting into. "At the end of the day, as the interviewer, I need to feel satisfied that the candidate has enough information on which to make a decision in case I make an offer," says Richard Kathnelson, VP of human resources at Syndesis, Inc., in Ontario, Canada. Open-ended questions that generate information-rich answers signal to Kathnelson that he is talking to a resourceful candidate who knows how to make informed decisions, a skill vital to any job.

A QUESTIONING ATTITUDE

Asking just the right questions is your chance to demonstrate that you are the best candidate for the job by communicating five different impressions:

- *Interest.* You have taken the trouble to investigate the job.
- *Intelligence.* You really understand the requirements of the job.
- *Confidence.* You have everything it takes to do to the job.
- *Personal appeal.* You are the type of person who will fit in well.
- *Assertiveness.* You ask for the job.

Of course, there is a sixth objective for your asking critical questions: to help you assess whether or not you really want the job. The job interview is a two-way street. You get to estimate the quality of the organization as much as the organizations gets to estimate your credentials.

The other important point is to avoid "What about me?" questions until after you get a job offer or a very strong expression of interest. "What about me?" questions are anything that goes to what the candidate receives as opposed to what the candidate offers. Remember, you have two roles in the interview: buyer and seller. For the first part of the interview, you are a seller. The only time you are buying is when they make you an offer.

Listen to Susan Trainer, senior information systems recruiter with RJS Associates in Hartford, Connecticut. She interviews hundreds of candidates to determine if they represent a good fit for her client companies. "It makes me crazy when I ask a candidate if they have any questions and they respond with either 'No, you have answered them already' or 'How many vacation days does your client give?'

"There are so many things you can screw up in a job interview, and not asking thoughtful questions when you have the opportunity is probably the biggest one. Interviewers want to know how candidates collect information, and the easiest way to know that is by listening to candidates ask questions," Trainer says.

"This is a real chance for a candidate to shine and set themselves apart from all the other job seekers. When I am prepping a candidate to go on an interview, I usually give them two or three very pointed questions to ask in the interview, and then we talk about another three for them to formulate," she adds. Her two favorites.

In what area could your team use a little polishing?

Why did you come to XZY Company?

"The questions you ask, and how you ask them, do as much to differentiate you from the competition as the questions asked by the interviewer," Trainer insists. As you prepare for the job interview, your questions have to be as carefully coordinated as your suit and shoes. If you miss the opportunity to leave your interviewer with any one of these impressions, you risk losing the main prize.

Thoughtful questions emphasize that you are taking an active role in the job selection process, not leaving the interviewer to do all the work. Active is good. Great questions demonstrate that, far from being a passive participant, you are action-oriented and engaged, reinforcing your interest in the job.

Asking questions is an excellent way to demonstrate your sophistication and qualifications. The questions you choose indicate your depth of knowledge of your field as well as your general level of intelligence. Asking questions also enables you to break down the formal interviewer-candidate relationship, establish an easy flow of conversation, and build trust and rapport. The matter of rapport is critical. Remember, most finalists for a job are more or less evenly matched in terms of qualifications. What gives the winning candidate the nod is rapport.

Your questions steer the interview the way you want it to go. Questions are a form of control. You can also use questions to divert an interviewer's line of questioning. If you sense the interviewer is leading up to a subject that you'd rather avoid—your job hopping, for example—ask a question about another topic. After a lengthy exchange, the interviewer might not return to her original line of questioning.

The more senior the position you are seeking, the more important it is to ask sophisticated and tough questions. Such questions demonstrate your understanding of the subtext and context of the position, as well as your confidence in challenging the interviewer. Hiring managers will judge you as much on the inquiries you make as on the responses you provide. If you don't ask sufficiently detailed questions, it will demonstrate lack of initiative and leadership qualities that a senior-level position demands.

CAN'T I JUST WING IT?

Imagine that tomorrow you are giving the senior decision makers in your organization the most important presentation of your career. Your future at the company literally depends on the outcome. Would you wing it?

Well, the situation I've just described is your next job interview. It's a presentation. The agenda: your future at the company. In the audience: the senior decision makers required to authorize offering you a position. Everyone is looking at you to shine. Now, given the stakes, are you willing to wing it? If you're comfortable with working like that, there's little need to read further.

Some applicants believe that spontaneity can make up for lack of strategic planning. But spontaneity, in cases such as this, can be indistinguishable from laziness and lack of preparation. Interviewers, professionals themselves, really want you to prepare for the interview as they did. Preparation is professionalism in action. It's common sense. It's courtesy. It works.

WRITE YOUR QUESTIONS DOWN

You've secured a job interview. Great. The first thing you do is homework (see Chapter 4 for a discussion on researching the company). The second thing you do is write down the questions you will ask.

Some job seekers are uncertain about whether they should write down their questions. If they do, should they bring them to the interview? The answer to both questions is yes. Doesn't that look, well, premeditated? Of course it does. That's the effect you want. See Chapter 5 for a fuller discussion of the issues around taking notes.

"I've always found that the most important thing at a job interview is to have a list of questions prepared before going in," says Kate Brothers, director of grants administration at Keuka College in Keuka Park, New York. "It accomplishes two things: It makes you look like you've done your homework, and it fills the awkward silences when the interviewer runs out of things to ask you. Also, it puts at least a portion of the interview in your control."

Writing down your questions accomplishes a number of useful objectives.

It helps articulate your thoughts. Your questions should be as crisp as your shirt or blouse. Write them down, practice reading them aloud, and edit until the questions sing.

It helps prioritize your issues. Not every question carries equal weight. But only when you write them all down can you decide which question to ask first. Some candidates write questions on index cards so they can easily order and reorder them until they have the flow they want.

It helps you remember. In the anxiety of the interview, you can easily forget a question you meant to ask. Or worse, your brain can vapor-lock and spill out something really dumb. If you have been interviewing with a number of companies, it is easy to forget where you are and ask a totally inappropriate question, such as asking about manufacturing facilities at an insurance company. Protect yourself and make yourself look professional by preparing questions in advance.

It improves your performance. Knowing which questions you will ask generally makes the interview go better. It breeds confidence. You will be able to guide the interview to highlight your qualifications in a way that your questions will underscore.

9

It makes you look prepared. That's a good thing as far as interviewers are concerned.

KNOW YOUR KILLER QUESTION

Depending on how the interview goes, you may have time to ask only one question. If that's the case, make it a killer question.

Everyone has a different killer question. Ask yourself, if you could present just one question, what would it be? Think about the brand you want to present. You are that brand. Take some time to think of the question that allows you to differentiate yourself from the crowd.

In many cases, the killer question has three elements:

• A statement that you appreciate the company's challenges or problem

• An assertion that you can solve the problem

• A request that you be given the opportunity to do so

The thoroughness with which you prepare for this question goes a long way in deciding whether you will be successful in getting a job offer.

Formulating open-ended, penetrating questions gives you a leg up on the competition. The right questions give the hiring manager a better picture of your value proposition to the company, the only basis on which you will be offered a position. The 15 rules that follow provide guidance to help you strategize about the questions you will take into your job interviews. Now is the time to be intentional about the interview, to take control, and to put your best foot forward.

15 RULES FOR FRAMING BETTER QUESTIONS

The art of asking questions is considering what responses you prefer and framing the questions to maximize your chances of getting the answers you want. Here are 15 rules for asking better questions.

1. Ask Open-Ended Questions

Closed-ended questions can be answered yes or no, and begin with words such as "did," "has," "does," "would," and "is." Open-ended questions—which usually begin with "how," "when," and "who"—create opportunities for a conversation and a much richer exchange of information. This is a closed-ended question:

CANDIDATE: Does the company have a child-care center on-site?

INTERVIEWER: Yes.

Here is an open-ended question:

CANDIDATE: How does the company support working parents?

INTERVIEWER: Let me show you a brochure about our award-winning day-care center located right here in the building. *Working Woman* recently rated it one of the top ten corporate day-care centers in the United States . . .

"Why" questions also start open-ended questions, but they often come off as too challenging in a job interview. See rule 8, below.

2. Keep It Short

Nothing is as disconcerting as a candidate spewing out a long, complicated question only to have the interviewer look confused and say, "I'm sorry. I don't understand your question." Restrict every question to one point. Resist mouthfuls like this:

I know that international sales are important, so how much of the company's revenues are derived from overseas, is that percentage growing, declining, or stable, do international tariffs present difficulties, and how will currency fluctuations impact the mix?

No interviewer should be expected to take on such a complicated question. If you really think a conversation about these points is in your interest, indicate your interest in the issue and then break the question into separate queries.

3. Don't Interrupt

Wait for the interviewer to finish the question. In other words, listen. Many candidates get anxious or impatient and jump in before the interviewer is finished asking the question. Sometimes they want to show off and demonstrate that they "get it."

Don't do it. The risks of flubbing outweigh any points you may get for appearing swift. To combat the tendency to interrupt, make sure the interviewer is really finished with each question. It's a good idea to pause three seconds before answering. If you can, use the time to think about what you want to say. In your mind's eye, repeat the question to yourself. Consider repeating it to the interviewer. See if you really have it. If not, ask the interviewer to repeat the question. Even if you can't make productive use of the three seconds, the pause will make you look thoughtful. The pause will also protect you from answering an incomplete question. For example, one candidate reported the following exchange:

HIRING MANAGER: I see by your résumé that you've had six systems analyst jobs in six years . . .

CANDIDATE [interrupting]: . . . And you want me to explain the job hopping, right?

HIRING MANAGER: Actually, I was going to ask what's one new skill you took away from each job. But since you mentioned job hopping, I am concerned about your ability to stick with one employer for more than year.

Oops. Better to wait for the full question.

How much better it would have been for the above candidate if the exchange had gone this way:

HIRING MANAGER: I see by your résumé that you've had six systems analyst jobs in six years. Can you mention one specific skill you took away from each experience?

CANDIDATE: You're asking what's one important skill I added to my portfolio from each of the jobs I've held, is that right?

HIRING MANAGER: Exactly.

CANDIDATE: Fair question. Let's take my jobs in order. At Netcom, I learned how to implement an enterprise network management strategy. Then at 4Com, I worked with client-side Java programming. I believe you mentioned Java as one of the hot buttons for this job. After that, I finally got my hands on . . .

4. Getting to Yes

James Joyce, the author of *Ulysses*, went out of his way to end his epic novel with a big "Yes," the most affirming word in the English language. He knew that ending the novel with "Yes" would let readers exit the novel with a positive frame of mind.

Your goal in the job interview is also to end the interview on an affirmation. In fact, the more yes's and statements of agreement you can generate, the better off you will be. Why? People, including job interviewers, really prefer being agreeable. Few people enjoy saying no. Who needs arguments? The best way to avoid arguments is to say yes.

If the job interview features wave after wave of yes's, think how much easier it will be for the interviewer to say yes to that last question, whether it's asked explicitly or implicitly:

I think I've demonstrated I'm qualified for this job. I'd very much like to join the team. Can we come to an agreement?

In tactical terms, that means framing your interview questions so the answers you want or expect will be positive. Here's an example of an exchange between a candidate and an interviewer to demonstrate the power of yes.

CANDIDATE: I have long been impressed by Acme Widgets. It's been the leader in pneumatic widgets for over 50 years, right?

INTERVIEWER: (proudly) Yes!

CANDIDATE: I noticed in the current annual report that the company sets aside $50 million, or 2.5 percent of revenues, for research and development. That's more than all of your competitors, isn't it?

INTERVIEWER: Yes. We lead the industry in allocation of R&D by revenue.

CANDIDATE: As the market for widgets gets more commoditized, we will have to differentiate the product, right? What specifically is the company doing to preserve the market share it has gained over the years?

As the interviewer answers the question, note the subtle messages the candidate is sending. The candidate ends each question with "right?" which invites the interviewer to answer with "yes." Of course, the candidate must be on sure ground. The candidate certainly wants to avoid any possibility that the interview will answer, "No, that's not quite right." Good research makes such questioning possible.

5. Use Inclusive Language

Look at the last dialogue again. Did you notice that the candidate subtly shifted from "you" to "we"? Words such as "we" and "our" subtly give the impression that the candidate is already a member of the team. The more comfortable the interviewer is with the concept of the candidate already being on the team, the better the candidate's chances. It's so much easier extending a job offer to someone whom the interviewer on some level already perceives as part of "us" instead of "them."

The risk, of course, is to come off as presumptuous. So a delicate touch with this technique is warranted. Generally, it works best later in the interview and after the interviewer has demonstrated a substantial level of interest in you. For example, if the company wants you to come back for a second (or third) interview. Of course, if the interviewer starts using inclusive language, you know that you are on safe ground and that an offer is in the cards.

6. Ask Questions the Interviewer Can Answer

Want to make interviewers defensive and uncomfortable? Ask them questions they don't know the answer to or can't answer because of confidentiality.

"Remember that although I do expect you to ask me some relevant questions, this isn't a game show," says Sonja Parker, VP of Integrated Design, Inc., in Ann Arbor, Michigan. "There isn't a prize for stumping me or asking the cleverest question. Just show me that you've given this opportunity some thought."

So as you formulate a question, think carefully about the content you are looking for as well as the person to whom you are addressing the question. In any case, avoid questions that reasonably intelligent people may not be expected to know. If the interviewer is asking you questions that you don't know the answer to, it may be tempting to try to stump the interviewer. Bad move. You may win the battle, but you will assuredly lose the war. Questions like this can't be expected to endear you to the interviewer:

CANDIDATE: Congress is considering an increase in the minimum wage. If it passes, do you believe that the microeconomic impacts of the minimum wage will be offset by the macroeconomic effects driven by the last round of cuts to the Federal Reserve discount rate?

INTERVIEWER: Huh?

Far from making you look smart, a question like this sets you up as an oddball. Even if you got a well-reasoned response to this question, of what possible use could it be to you as you evaluate the position? Let go of any competitiveness or urgency to show off.

At all times, know to whom you are talking. Asking a hiring manager detailed questions about medical insurance options is not useful. Nor is asking the human resources interviewer questions about the fine points of the company's virtual private network. Finally, be careful to avoid trespassing on confidential information, especially if you are currently employed by a competitor.

As long as you are at it, stay away from cage-rattling questions. These are questions that some interviewers may throw at you, but they cannot win you points if you throw them back at the interviewer. I provided a list of some of these shake-'em-up questions in *The Manager's Book of Questions: 751 Great Questions for Hiring the Best Person*. In this category fall hypothetical questions (any questions that begin with the word "if") and probing questions of all sorts. Examples of questions that you should leave at home:

If you could forge an alliance with any organization in the world, which one would it be?

What unwritten rules at work make it difficult to get things done quickly, efficiently, or profitably?

You're the corporate weatherperson; what's your forecast for the organization using meteorological terms?

Don't get me wrong. These can be great questions. And if you could get an honest answer out of them, I might say toss one or two out there and see what happens. But if you ask questions such as these before you get an offer, it has the effect of raising the ante too high. No one wants to work that hard. The interviewer will simply fold and hope the next candidate is less challenging.

7. Avoid Questions That Are Obvious or Easy to Determine

Asking questions such as these will make you look uninformed or lazy:

What does IBM stand for?

Who is the company's chief executive officer?

Where is the company located?

Does the company have a Web site?

Why? Because the answers are as close as the company's Web site or annual report. Don't ask the interviewer to state the obvious or do your job for you. At best it will raise questions about your ability to engage, and at worst it will cost you the job offer.

8. Avoid "Why" Questions

"Why" questions—queries that start with "why"—often come off as confrontational. Interviewers can get away with asking you "why" questions. After all, they are interested in your thought processes and the quality of your decisions. But when the situation is reversed, "why" questions from the job seeker sometimes make the interviewer defensive. Not good:

Why did you consolidate the Seattle and Dallas manufacturing facilities?

It comes off as a challenge. Better:

I am interested in the company's recent decision to consolidate the Seattle and Dallas manufacturing facilities. In a **Wall Street Journal** *article, your CEO stated the wisdom of keeping manufacturing facilities close to customers whenever possible. Yet this move creates distance be-*

tween the company and some of its customers. Can we talk about this de-cision for a moment?

9. Avoid Asking Questions That Call for a Superlative

Questions that call for a superlative ("What is the best book of all time?") make people hesitate and also put them on the defensive. When faced with a superlative, the interviewer's mind gets vapor-locked and he or she hesitates.

Poor: What is the biggest challenge for the company/team?

Better: What do you see as three important challenges for the company/team?

Poor: What is the absolute best thing about this company?

Better: What are a couple of things you really like about the company?

Avoiding superlatives gives the interviewer wiggle room to answer questions more personally.

10. Avoid Leading or Loaded Questions

Leading questions signal the interviewer that you are looking for a specific answer. They also signal that you are, at best, an awkward communicator and, at worst, manipulative. In any case, skewing questions is not in your interest. Be on guard that your questions are phrased to be impartial. For example, this is a leading question:

Isn't it true that your company is regarded as paying slightly better than average?

This attempt to box in the interviewer is so transparent it will backfire. Keep the question straight:

How do your company's compensation schedules compare with the in-dustry average?

The wording of this next question is arrogant and makes you look foolish.

I'm sure you agree with the policy that the customer is always right. How are employees rewarded for going out of their way to put the customer first?

What gives you the right to assume what the interviewer agrees with? Ask it straight. There's no harm in reporting a part of a company's positive reputation, if it's true.

The company has a reputation for excellent customer service. How do you motivate and empower employees to make exceptional customer service a priority?

Loaded questions also make you look bad. Loaded questions reveal your prejudices and biases. Besides being out of place in a job interview, such questions convey a sense of arrogance or even contempt. They make you look like a bully. They always backfire on you, no matter how much you think your interviewer shares your biases. Typical loaded questions might be:

How can the company justify locating manufacturing plants in the People's Republic of China with its miserable record of human rights violations?

With all the set-aside programs for minorities and people who weren't even born in this country, what progress can a white American man hope to have in your company?

Questions like these reveal your biases, often unintentionally, and cannot advance your candidacy.

11. Avoid Veiled Threats

Interviewers hate to be bullied, and they will send you packing at the first hint of a threat. That means if you have another job offer from company A, keep it to yourself until after company B has expressed an interest in making you an offer as well. Unfortunately, candidates have abused the tactic of pitting employers against each other by brandishing genuine or, as is more likely the case, fictitious job offers. A few years ago, this tactic created an unreasonable and unsustainable climate for hiring. Don't test it with today's crop of interviewers; they will wish you luck with the other company and never look back. For example:

I'm considering a number of other offers, including a very attractive one from your main competitor, and need to make a decision by Friday. Can I have your best offer by then?

This question smacks of bullying and desperation. It's hard to come up with alternative wording, but this is more effective:

Everything I know about your company and the opportunity you described leads me to believe that I can immediately start adding value. I would very much welcome receiving an offer. Another company has made me an attractive offer to join them, and I said I would give them my decision by Friday. If my application is receiving serious consideration here, I would very much like to consider it before then. Is that possible?

12. Avoid Questions That Hint of Desperation

There is a line from the movie *Broadcast News* that applies to job seekers: "Wouldn't this be a great world if terror and desperation were attractive qualities?" Unfortunately, job interviewers, like partners in romance, recoil at displays of desperation. Employers don't want to know about your financial plight, any more than they want to hear about your failing romances. You must avoid any hint of discouragement when a job offer is not immediately forthcoming. By all means avoid:

I simply must have this job. My rent is late, and my wife and I are going to be out on the street if you don't make me an offer.

Even a hiring manager sympathetic to your plight cannot afford to continue the interview. This next question is also too desperate:

I had hoped that my interview would be so good that you'd offer me a job. What did I do wrong?

The only attitude of a candidate that really makes sense is relaxed confidence.

13. Asking Questions That Focus on What the Company Can Do for You

The hiring manager is less interested in how much you want to better yourself than what you can do to ease his or her problem. "What about me?" questions like this are a turnoff:

I'm very committed to developing my intellectual property by learning new technologies. What kinds of tuition benefits and other educational support can I expect?

It's nice that you want to improve yourself, but the hiring manager is not interested in your commitment to education on his time. He has a problem to solve and wants to know if you can help solve it. If you can, maybe then the company can invest in your skills so you can solve even more of its problems. Compare the above question to:

I want to put all my experience and everything I know in the service of solving the challenges you have outlined. At the same time, I hope to increase my value to the company by learning new skills and technologies. Does the company have any programs that help me add value by learning new skills?

14. If You Want the Job, Ask for It

We explore the issue of asking for the job in Chapter 12, but it is so important that I include a preview here. As a candidate, you should use your opportunity to ask questions as a platform to ask for the job. These are called bid-for-action questions because, like every marketer (in this case, you), you should conclude every contact with the prospect (the hiring manager) with an invitation to take an action (make me an offer).

Many employers feel that a desire for the position is just as important as the ability to do the job. A very effective interviewing technique is simply to ask for the job. One way to do this is to ask the employer:

Do you think I can do the job?

Generally, the interviewer will hedge. But if the answer is yes, smile and say:

Great! When do you want me to start?

More likely, the interviewer will say something like:

I am very impressed with your credentials, but we have a number of other steps to go though before I can give you an answer to that question.

That's fine. It's also possible the interviewer will state some objections. Believe it or not, that's even better. An unstated objection will kill your chances every time. With stated objections, at least, you have the possibility of reversing the concern.

Of course, there are some objections that you really can't do much about:

The job listing clearly noted that the position requires a minimum of six years of object-oriented coding experience. You don't have any.

Some objections are softer:

I'm concerned that you are not as seasoned in leading large multidisciplinary teams as this position requires.

Here you have some recourse:

I can see how you might get that impression. But if I can take you back to my work for XYZ Company, I showed you how I led four separate teams. What I might not have emphasized is that I coordinated the teams. At the height of the project, there were 65 developers across the four teams all reporting to me in a matrix structure. In the end, under my supervision, the teams succeeded in launching a strategic product on time and on budget. Does that speak to your concern?

Note how the candidate checks out if the response moderated the objection. If not, try again.

Even if your experience is light in some area, it may not be fatal. Try to find out what percentage of the job that requirement represents. Then attack the gap head-on with something like:

I am willing to put in extra time to come up to speed in this area. Would that help?

If so, ask for the job:

21

I understand the challenges of the job, and I believe I have the experience to take them on. I would very much like to start doing this important work.

Before leaving the interview, thank the employer for taking the time to talk to you about the position. Follow up with a personal thank you note to the employer, stating once again why you'd be an asset to the company and expressing your interest in the position.

15. Don't Ask Questions That Are Irrelevant to the Job or Organization

Another awkward moment comes when the interviewer challenges your question with something like, "Now, why on earth would you want to know that?"

In the same way that you can respond to interviewer's illegal questions with, "I fail to see what that question has to do with my ability to do the job," don't give the interviewer an excuse to apply a similar phrase to your question. To be safe, make sure that every question can pass this test: Does the answer the question elicits shed light on the job, the company, and its desirability as a workplace? If not, the question is irrelevant.

Also, stay away from marginal queries about competitors, other positions that don't relate to the position you're interviewing for, or current trends that have no bearing on the organization.

While asking about the interviewer's individual experience at the company is okay (see Chapter 2), try not to interrogate the interviewer about his or her career history. It's okay, for example, to ask specific questions about what the interviewer likes best and least about working at the organization, but don't go beyond that. If the interviewer chooses to share some in-depth information about his or her career path or experiences at the organization, then feel free to ask follow-up questions. Just keep them open-ended and don't push it.

What Do Interviewers Want?
Key Traits Employers Use to Assess Fit

Thinking—can the candidate:

- Quickly and effectively solve challenging problems?
- Learn and apply new job-related information?
- Develop sophisticated long-term strategic responses?

Planning—can the candidate:

- Plan time and projects without missing any steps or deadlines?
- Follow multiple rules exactly without exception?
- Act deliberately without analysis paralysis?
- Execute ruthlessly and with precision?

Interacting—can the candidate:

- Demonstrate effective leadership ability?
- Get along with others in a very close-knit working environment?
- Effectively deal with customer demands on a regular basis?
- Demonstrate genuine support and concern for the welfare of others?
- Be outgoing and socially expressive?
- Effectively coach and develop skills of coworkers?
- Be persuasive in a low-key manner?

Motivation—can the candidate:

- Be on time without missing workdays?
- Frequently suggest new ideas or job improvements?
- Work long hours without complaint?
- Cheerfully do more than what's required for the job?
- Be flexible and accepting of frequent changes?
- Be visibly supportive of the organization?

CHAPTER 2

QUESTIONS YOU SHOULD NEVER INITIATE

DON'T GO THERE

This book is focused on helping you to identify and customize questions that will help you look good in the interview and secure a job offer. To that end, an almost boundless universe of questions about the job, the company, and the industry awaits you.

But there is set of questions that you should generally avoid initiating until two things are true. First, the interviewer initiates them (and sometimes not even then). Second, you have either the job offer in hand or a serious commitment of interest from your prospective employer.

Remember, your goal is to get a job offer. These are questions that cannot help you advance this agenda, but could seriously derail your efforts. Some of these questions are important, and you should definitely ask them, but not now.

COMPENSATION

With few exceptions, it is never in your interest to initiate questions about salary and related compensation issues such as benefits, vacation, and holidays. No matter how you frame the questions, you come off looking greedy and fixated on what the company can do for you instead of what you can do for the company. Any discussion about these issues will distract the interviewer from your qualifications and how you can help the company.

Yes, money and benefits are important. I guarantee you will have this conversation after the company expresses an interest in you. Your bargaining position will be much stronger then, so just resist asking about money and concentrate on showing that you understand the company's challenges and can help solve them.

On the other hand, let's be real. Money is critical, so why should it be so awkward to acknowledge that fact? True, most career counselors and job-hunting experts suggest it is taboo for you to ask about pay before the interviewer does, but I think it's possible to be too rigid on this point. Occasionally it may make sense for the candidate to initiate a relaxed conversation about pay issues at an early point in the interview. Any reasonable person would expect rate of pay, health benefits, and what constitutes the workweek to be important topics. To pointedly ignore them diminishes the honesty of the relationship between the candidate and the interviewer, surely not an auspicious way to start a relationship with someone who may become your immediate supervisor and mentor.

There is one exception when issues of pay should come first, not last. That exception refers to salespeople who are paid by commission, not salary. With salespeople, the acknowledged desire to earn a high income is considered an unalloyed virtue. Companies actually like to see a reasonable level of greediness in their salespeople. The system is set up so that salespeople make money only if they earn the company a lot more money. Thus if you are interviewing for a sales job, it can be appropriate for you to raise the issue of commissions, royalties, quotas, and other compensation issues early on in the interview.

SELF-LIMITING QUESTIONS

These are questions that appear to put your needs before those of the employer. You may have legitimate issues around matters of hours, transportation, medical requirements, education, and accommodations of all sorts. But it is rarely to your advantage to initiate these issues before the employer has expressed an interest in you. Rather, wait until you have indications of real interest from the employer. The interviewer will eventually ask you a question such as, "Are there any other issues we should know about before taking the next step?" It's at that point you can more safely bring up the issues you have in mind.

In other words, be sure that the question you ask doesn't raise barriers or objections. For example:

Is relocation a necessary part of the Job?

The very question raises doubts about your willingness to relocate. Even if the person selected for the position is not tracked for relocation, the negativity of the question makes the hiring manager wonder whether you are resistant in other areas as well.

If the issue of relocation is important to you, by all means ask, but go with a phrasing that reinforces your flexibility, not challenges it:

I'm aware that relocation is often required in a career and I am prepared to relocate for the good of the company as necessary. Could you tell me how often I might be asked to relocate in a five- or ten-year period?

Here are a few more examples of self-limiting questions and the comments of recruiters who fielded them:

Is job-sharing a possibility?

Possibly, but does this mean you can't give us a commitment for full-time work?

Can you tell me whether you have considered the incredible benefits of telecommuting for this position?

Why do you want to get out of the office before you have even seen it?

I understand that employee paychecks are electronically deposited. Can I get my paycheck in the old-fashioned way?

You are already asking for exceptions. What's next? And are you afraid of technology?

I won't have to work for someone with less education than I have, will I?

You clearly have a chip on your shoulder. Why should we take a chance that you don't have other interpersonal issues?

The job description mentions weekend work. Are you serious?
We're serious about the job description. We're suddenly less serious about you.

You get the picture. Don't raise red flags. Once the interviewer has decided that you are the right person for the job, you will find the employer to be much more accommodating about issues like these. Wait until after you have the offer in hand before you raise these questions.

WHAT ABOUT HUMOR?

Charles Handler, today the head of Rocket-hire.com, recounts this object lesson. Interviewing for a recruiting job with the company's CEO, Handler was trying to make a point about the most reliable methods of selecting employees. In an attempt to be lighthearted, Handler said that he supported every way of selecting employees except graphology. Graphology is the study of handwriting as a means of analyzing character.

You can guess what happened next. The CEO looked up with a tight smile and slowly informed Handler that graphology was his hobby and that he thought the practice had substantial merit.

The good news is at the end of the day, the wisecrack didn't hurt Handler. He still received a job offer. But it did teach him a lesson. "Think twice about making a joke or a wisecrack," he says. "Any subject you choose, no matter how seemingly innocuous, has the potential for alienating the interviewer."

On the other hand, humor elegantly framed and sharply focused can be effective and advantageous. But it must come naturally to you. Nothing is as risky as forced humor. Amateurs shouldn't try this at the office. A half-baked attempt at humor can seriously backfire on you, and if you offend the interviewer—a possibility less and less discountable in these politically correct times—you will never recover. For that reason many job coaches advise against any attempt at humor, sarcasm, or teasing. Just play it straight, they say, and you can't go wrong.

Some hiring managers welcome humor because it demonstrates you can keep work in a proper perspective. "The ability to laugh at yourself is a great attribute," says Susan Trainer. "It means you don't take your-self too seriously, which is a very attractive trait."

Other recruiters are skeptical. "I want my questions taken seriously," warns Bryan Debenport, corporate recruiter at Alcon Laboratories, a 3000-employee manufacturer of ophthalmic products in Fort Worth, Texas. "Humor may be appropriate at the start and finish of interviews, but use it sparingly."

The goal of using humor is to bond with the interviewer, to use your shared senses of humor as a way to underscore the prospect that you will fit into the organization. Of course, if your perspective and that of the hiring manager seriously differ, then your attempt at humor will only un-derscore the disconnect.

At the same time, when people laugh, certain physiological changes take place that make people more flexible, relaxed, and—this is what you most want—agreeable. Humor is also synonymous with wit—and wit is born of intelligence. No wonder recruiters look for candidates with this quality. Let the interviewer set the tone. If the interviewer starts with a joke and seems to be in good humor, you can try for a little self-deprecating humor.

MAKE FUN ONLY OF YOURSELF

The only thing you can make fun of is yourself. Everything else, with-out exception, is off limits. You may think you and the recruiter share a perspective on politics, gender relations, and certain ethnic groups. Don't go there. No laugh is worth insulting someone. There's always a risk of humor backfiring. If you think there's the slightest chance of of-fending someone, keep the humor to yourself.

So what kinds of self-deprecating joking can pass the humor test? Di-alect is too risky. Leave it at home. Sarcasm may be misinterpreted. Deep-six it. Personal anecdotes can sometimes work. But make them personal, short, and to the point. One candidate reports that the follow-ing line, delivered tongue in cheek with a broad smile, sometimes led to a laugh and real feedback:

How do you like me so far?

A line like this can work, concedes Nancy Levine, VP of client serv-ices at San Francisco–based Pacific Firm, but the risks are too high because it is so obviously a line. "If I happen to feel that the candidate and I have created a close rapport, that our senses of humor are on the same wavelength, then it's great. But there is nothing more irritating to me than someone trying to be funny whom I don't find funny. Proceed with caution if you want to use humor. And then, use it sparingly, just to add spice, like pepper on the finest filet mignon."

Another candidate got some mileage out of a similar expression, by finding just the right time in the interview to say, in a dead-on New York City accent:

As Ed Koch used to say, "How'm I doing?"
(Ed Koch is a former mayor of New York who managed by walking around the city and offering that phrase in order to get feedback from citizens.)

How about jokes? Is it ever useful to tell a joke in a job interview?

Jokes are probably too risky, but it may pay to memorize a couple just in case. I know one HR director who is known to ask candidates to tell him a joke as a test of how nimble the candidate's mind is. Every once in a while—perhaps if the interview is at a more informal setting such as a restaurant—it may make sense to offer a joke. The quasi-social nature of the event might allow for more flexibility. But even here I urge caution.

Some interviewers will tell you a joke, either to break the ice or to illustrate a point. Occasionally, unprepared or unprofessional interviewers tell jokes because they are uncomfortable or don't know what else to do. In either case, resist the temptation to create a false rapport by exchanging jokes. It doesn't advance the interview, and little good can come of it. Do listen to the subtext of the joke and come back with a question that indicates the joke gave you a serious insight into the situation:

I appreciate the way you said that. It's true, isn't it, that communication breakdowns come in the most unexpected ways. And while it can sometimes be funny, communication breakdowns impose real costs on the organization. Companywide intranets offer real benefits to cross-departmental communications. At my last job, I led the team that developed ...

If you must tell a joke, make sure it is short and pokes fun at yourself or some general issue of work. If it's about the job interviewing process, so much the better. Never tell more than one joke, no matter how much you are coaxed. This joke, for example, has made the rounds of the HR chat boards.

> Reaching the end of a job interview, the human resources person asked a young engineer fresh out of MIT what kind of a salary he was looking for.
> "In the neighborhood of $140,000 a year, depending on the benefits package."
> "Well, what would you say to a package of five weeks vacation, 14 paid holidays, full medical and dental, company-matching retirement fund to 50 percent of salary, and a company car leased every 2 years . . . say, a red Corvette?"
> "Wow! You're kidding!" the young engineer said.
> "Yeah, but you started it."

Five Rules for Using Humor

1. Poke fun at yourself only, nothing else.
2. Follow the interviewer's lead.
3. Don't force it.
4. No sarcasm at any time.
5. If in doubt, don't.

QUESTIONS ABOUT THE INTERVIEWER

Because individuals relate to individuals, it's natural that applicants want to know about the interviewer. The interviewer also happens to be the most immediate representative of the company they hope to join. Is it appropriate to ask questions about the interviewer's history, opinions, and experience?

Absolutely. People like to talk to people. Most applicants want to know about the interviewer. One big question is how personal can you get without crossing the line? "Asking questions about the interviewer is fine if you keep the questions relevant and focused on the job," says Bob

Conlin, VP of marketing at Incentive Systems in Bedford, Massachusetts. Conlin says he is often asked questions such as:

What convinced you to come to Incentive Systems?

What are some of the best attributes of Incentive Systems?

Behavioral questions very similar to the type candidates are asked are also fair game to ask the interviewer, says Melanie Mays, president of Empyrean Consulting, a recruiting consulting firm in Dallas, Texas. These questions are best asked after a mutual interest has been established. They should go only to the individual with whom you might be working:

Can you tell me about a project that was successful and how you accomplished it as a team?

Can you tell me about a time when you encountered constraints and how you resolved them?

How do you think your employees would describe your management style?

Some hiring managers are perfectly comfortable with such questions, but others might get defensive, Mays warns. If that's the case, back off, although the defensiveness itself will give you a clue about the situation. Other personal questions to consider asking the interviewer:

Tell me about your career choice. How did you get into recruiting? What attracted you to this organization?

What are some of the things you especially admire about the company?

If you could change some things about the company, what would they be?

How many layers of management are there between you and the CEO?

When was the last time you had contact with the CEO?

Avoid questions that are over the line. Personal questions that are clearly inappropriate would be ones such as:

Are you single?

How much money do you take home?

What would it take for you to leave your job?

Would you want to work for the guy I might be working for?

What's the worst thing you got away with at this company?

Aren't you a little young (or old) to be in your position?

"I welcome questions about my personal experience that give me an opportunity to share my enthusiasm about the company," says Beau Harris, a recruiter at Handspring, Inc., the Mountain View, California–based manufacturer of the Visor personal digital assistant. What questions would Harris resent? "There are a whole range of questions about marital status, religion, political views that I as an interviewer am not allowed to ask," he says. "I believe the candidate should be held to the same standard. Questions like that should not be part of the decision-making mix."

YES, THERE REALLY ARE DUMB QUESTIONS

A platitude popular in educational circles is that there is no such thing as a dumb question. After talking to hundreds of recruiters and job coaches around the world, I can tell you that, unfortunately, there really are dumb questions, and their articulation has cost thousands of people jobs for which they might otherwise have been qualified. Job candidates ask dumb questions every day. These questions prove they haven't done their homework, haven't listened, or have a tin ear for context.

ALL-TIME DEAL-KILLING QUESTIONS

Candidates who ask these questions remain candidates.

These questions basically terminated the job interview, according to recruiters, job coaches, and staffing professionals who generously shared the worst questions candidates asked in job interviews. This list doesn't include "Do you drug-test?" (four instances) and requests for dates (six instances).

There seem to be no conditions that justify asking the following questions in any circumstances:

- Is it possible for me to get a small loan?
- What is it that your company does?
- Can I see the break room?
- Are you (the interviewer) married?
- What are your psychiatric benefits?
- How many warnings do you get before you are fired?
- Do you provide employees with gun lockers?
- Can you guarantee me that I will still have a job here a year from now?
- Do I get to keep the frequent-flier miles from company trips?
- Would anyone notice if I came in late and left early?
- How many (insert name of ethnic group) do you have working here?
- What does this company consider a good absenteeism record?
- Can you tell me about your retirement plan?
- The job description mentions weekend work. Are you serious?
- What is the zodiac sign of the company president?
- You're not going to check my references, are you?
- Is it easy to get away with stuff around here?
- Do I have to work more than 40 hours a week?
- Why do I have to fill out this job application? It's all on my résumé.
- How do you define sexual harassment?
- Can the company buy 5,000 copies of my wife's book?
- Am I allowed smoking breaks?
- Will my office be near an ice machine?
- I missed my lunch. Do you mind if I eat my sandwich while we talk?
- I hope this doesn't take too long. My mother is waiting for me in the car.
- When will I be eligible for my first vacation?

CHAPTER 3

WHEN TO QUESTION

NO NEED TO WAIT FOR
AN INVITATION

While the common pattern is to have the interviewer invite the job seeker to ask questions, you are sometimes better off taking the initiative. Here are three scenarios in which asking questions (after you ask permission to ask them) gives you better control of the job interview.

IN THE BEGINNING

Janice Brookshier, a Seattle-based recruiting contractor and president of Seattlejobs.org, has an informal interviewing style. In her dialogue with the candidate, she makes it quite clear that the candidate is free to ask questions at any point in the conversation. Brookshier notes, "Candidates are always free to ask a question, whether solicited or not."

If Brookshier doesn't get intelligent questions during the first part of the interview, she starts to wonder. But her worst suspicions are confirmed if the candidate doesn't have any questions even after she invites some. "I see it as a test," she says. "If you have no questions for me, it tells me that you are either way too passive or just not very serious. Either way, I lose interest real quickly."

What impresses Brookshier the most are questions that transform a question that she had asked the candidate earlier in the interview. For example, if she had asked the candidate:

What accomplishments in your career are you most proud of?

or

Can you tell me about your greatest weakness?

Brookshier would be impressed by a candidate who countered with:

What accomplishments in its history is the company most proud of?

or

Can you tell me about the company's greatest weakness?

THE PREEMPTIVE QUESTION

If you really want to assert yourself and take complete control of the interview, there is a compelling question that will transform the interview. This question is best used if your interviewer is the actual hiring manager, or the person with hiring authority. It is less useful with screeners. The question is:

By what criteria will you select the person for this job?

This marvelous question, recommended by Irv Zuckerman in his book *Hire Power*, lets the candidate effectively seize control of the interview in a way that many interviewers find reassuring. Here's a typical exchange (with comments) between an interviewer and a candidate:

INTERVIEWER: Thank you for coming. Can I get you a cup of coffee?

CANDIDATE: No, thank you. Perhaps later. (Leaving the door open softens the refusal to accept the interviewer's hospitality. Avoid anything that might spill. Also you will need your hands free for taking notes on the important information you are about to receive.)

INTERVIEWER: Well, then, make yourself comfortable. Can you tell me about yourself?

CANDIDATE: I'll be glad to. But first, may I ask a question? (Always ask permission.)

INTERVIEWER: Of course. (You will never be refused. The interviewer is now curious about what you are going to ask.)

36

CANDIDATE: My question is this: By what criteria will you select the person for this job?

INTERVIEWER: That's a good question.

CANDIDATE: Is it all right if I take notes? (Always ask permission.)

INTERVIEWER: Of course. Now, let me see. I think the first criterion is . . .

Now listen. When the interviewer is done reviewing the first criterion, ask about the second. Then the third. Pretty soon you will have a list of the interviewer's hot buttons, a recipe for the ideal candidate for the job. Your challenge is to underscore how your credentials and experience just happen to fall in perfect alignment with those very criteria.

Let's back up a minute. Notice what else you have accomplished by asking this marvelous question. You have seized control of the interview. Suddenly the interviewer is working according to *your* agenda. The question—*by what criteria will you select the person for this job*—is designed to put you in the driver's seat. Play with the wording at your own risk. Look at how the question parses:

By what criteria. This part of the question focuses the discussion where it belongs—on the job and its requirements, rather than your education, experience, age, gender, etc. What the hiring manager really wants is someone who can do the job and will fit in. Are you that someone? Can you prove it? That's your goal in the next phases of the interview.

will you select. This acknowledges the authority of the decision maker. It is critical for you to know if, by chance, you are talking to someone who is not the decision maker, but merely a gatekeeper. In either case, you need to focus on the action verb in the clause and what you must provide in order to be selected.

the person. Only one person will be selected for this particular job. You want that person to be you. One of your jobs in the interview is to remind the hiring manager that you are a well-rounded, likable person who will fit in with the other people in the organization.

for this job. This phrase underscores the idea that the subject of this conversation is a job that the interviewer needs to fill because a vital organizational function is not being done. Furthermore, the ideal remedy for the problem is available and ready to start.

BEFORE THE BEGINNING

A job interview can be over before you think it's even started. In other words, a job interview can be a conversation that starts long before the first word comes out of your mouth.

This scenario demonstrates what a mistake it is to assume that you can time the start of a job interview.

Susan arrived early at her job interview. At the appointed hour, Susan's interviewer greeted her and asked her to follow him to his office. Susan immediately noticed that the interviewer seemed a bit befuddled, as if he forgot where the office was. As they started walking through a maze of cubicles, he seemed to hesitate, looking first left and then right. Ignoring Susan, he paused at every intersection, like he was a pioneer exploring a territory for the first time. With Susan in tow, he even retraced his steps a couple of times. Susan felt very uncomfortable, but she didn't know what to do. Should she say anything? Would a comment offend him? Maybe the interviewer had a disability of some sort. So she hung back and waited for the interviewer to act. Eventually, they found their way to the interview room where the interviewer asked Susan a few perfunctory questions before thanking her for coming. Susan did not get an offer.

What went on here? If you were Susan, how would you have handled the situation? Before reading further, take a minute to consider the challenge, because that's exactly what it was.

Susan didn't realize it, but the maze-running was part of the job interview. By the time the interviewer got to the talking part, the interview was over and the candidate had been eliminated. Yes, it might seem sleazy, but the interviewer played incompetent to test Susan's leadership qualities. Would she offer to help? Would she take an active role in some way, offering whatever skills she could muster for the occasion? Or would she remain passive? *The interviewer was hoping that Susan would ask a question.* The most important part of the interview took place before the candidate thought anything important happened.

What could Susan have done? The first thing is, she should have recognized that she was being tested. In fact, all candidates do well to assume that as soon as they leave their house, they are being evaluated. What are some things Susan could have done or said? A job coach in Dallas whose clients have encountered this technique suggests one approach.

> Well, there's no right or wrong here. But I'd have coached Susan to do something to acknowledge what is, after all, an uncomfortable situation. If I'm recruiting for a team leader or manager, I look for candidates who are authentic, who offer to help in some way, or at least use humor to diffuse the tension. One candidate made me laugh when she joked, "Maybe we should leave a trail of bread crumbs so we can find our way back!" Mostly I want to see evidence that the candidate is thinking. What makes me hesitate is when candidates don't have a clue about what to do or are too timid to do it.

Thankfully, techniques like these are falling out of favor, so you probably won't encounter too many role-playing techniques. But the point remains: The interview starts sooner than you think. Keep thinking and don't hesitate to ask questions. Here's another scenario you might encounter.

> Charles was interviewing for a senior sales position, and everything was going perfectly. His experience was exactly right, and Charles and the hiring manager, the VP of sales, seemed to be getting along great. So imagine the candidate's surprise when the interviewer suddenly stood up and said, "I'm sorry, Charles. I just don't think it's going to work out after all. Thank you for meeting with me and good luck to you." The rejection came so unexpectedly Charles that could only mumble something as he walked out.

What's going on here? Again, take a minute to put yourself in Charles's shoes. How would you have handled the situation?

39

Charles didn't realize it, but the resistance from the recruiter signaled the start of the job interview, not the end. Remember, Charles was being sized up for a senior sales position. A critical skill for such a position is grace in handling a prospect's objections or rejection. So the interviewer threw a big objection at the candidate to see how he would react.

What could Charles have done? One *Fortune* 500 recruiter suggests Charles could have responded:

> Excuse me, can I just have another minute? I'm confused. I thought the interview was going pretty well and that my experience fit the position you described very closely. Apparently, I missed something important. I would very much like to understand where I saw a disconnect between my skills and the job so that I might have the opportunity to demonstrate that I really am the best candidate for the job.

"This kind of response would tell me that Charles can handle objections, accepts responsibility for not making his case, and asks for information so that he may continue selling, which is why I'm hiring him," the recruiter adds. In short, Charles needed a bid-for-action question, as described in Chapter 12.

AT THE END

This is the typical point at which you'll be invited to ask any questions you may have. The interviewer will lean back and turn the interview over to you. It may seem like the interview is coming to an end. It's not. Interviewers are unanimous on this: They really expect you to ask intelligent questions.

Don't assume you know when the interview is over. The safest bet is to apply this rule: The interview is not over until *you* no longer have an interest in the job. Until then, the clock is ticking.

CHAPTER 4

DO YOUR HOMEWORK

KNOW BEFORE YOU ASK

When Sonja Parker interviews a candidate, she expects that the job seeker will have done a reasonable amount of research into the company. Before you interview with Parker, VP of Integrated Design in Ann Arbor, Michigan, you will receive a folder with general information on the company, a detailed job overview, and an application. During the preliminary telephone interview, Parker always asks:

What do you know about us? Have you reviewed the packet I sent, or have you poked around on our Web site?

If the candidate hedges, Parker questions whether she should invite the candidate in for a job interview. If the candidate answers yes, Parker asks:

What is your impression of what we do?

"I want to see if the candidate can articulate the information about our company and the job," she says. Her reasons for asking are twofold. First, she wants some feedback on how effectively the company's recruiting materials are working. But even more importantly, she believes that a candidate who has taken the time to thoroughly study the recruiting materials demonstrates real interest in the job, while one who has not is a poor risk.

"If you want to work at Integrated Design, I insist that you demonstrate at least a basic understanding of what the company does," she

41

says. The best way to demonstrate that is to ask Parker informed questions, such as:

I've scanned your Web site and the materials you sent me. I understand that Integrated Design specializes in employee data integration. As a service business, has the recent economic downturn changed the weight of the build-versus-buy calculation that every customer must evaluate?

Such a question tells Parker that the candidate not only researched the company's mission but has a mature understanding of the challenges of a service company. On the other hand, Parker experiences a visceral turn-off for applicants who show no evidence they looked at the recruitment information packet she sent about the company. She also has no use for applicants who expect her to repeat all the information contained in the information packet. Such applicants—they hardly rise to the status of candidates—are too unmotivated to get Parker's attention.

"If candidates ask no questions at all, especially after I sent them an information packet of recruitment materials, I know they are cruising," agrees Bob Conlin, VP of marketing at Incentive Systems in Bedford, Massachusetts. "If a candidate tells me she is considering committing the next phase of her career to Incentive Systems, I want to know she is thinking hard about the opportunity. I expect to hear some very probing questions."

One of the strongest candidates in Conlin's experience was prepared not only with great questions, but with a portfolio of materials the candidate could point to during the interview. The candidate for a senior marketing position had copies of Incentive Systems' company's data sheets and full-page ads and those of its competitors. Using these materials, the candidate asked informed questions about the merits of specific marketing campaigns on behalf of specific products. "As soon as he pulled out the portfolio, I said to myself, 'This is my guy!'" Conlin recalls.

START WITH THE COMPANY'S WEB SITE

In the age of the Internet, there is absolutely no excuse for you not to have excellent information about a company. All public companies and most private companies have Web sites. The Web sites are free and available 24 hours a day. You can access the Web sites from any computer connected to the Internet. If you don't have a computer, go to the library or an Internet café. Log onto the company's Web site. It has all the information you could want to frame thoughtful and impressive questions. "If a candidate can't spend 15 minutes on my company's Web site," Conlin notes, "it immediately tells me that they are, at best, not serious and, at worst, just plain lazy."

A company's Web site also gives you good clues about whether the organization is growing or struggling.

The Web site addresses of most companies are obvious. At the place in the browser where it says "address," just type in "www" (for World Wide Web), the name of the company, and the extension ".com." Most Web addresses are obvious. For example, Cisco Systems is *www.cisco.com*. General Motors is *www.gm.com*. General Electric is *www.ge.com*.

Another way to find a Web site is to use a search engine. I prefer Google, although there are dozens of general and specialized search engines that will do the job. Simply type in *www.google.com* and the lean page of the Google Web site will appear. In the blank box, type in the name of the company you want to research and click on "I'm feeling lucky." Google will almost always take you straight to the Web site you want. It's unlikely that Google will fail you, but if it does, click "Back" and then click on the "Search Google" button. Now you will get a list of possible destinations. The company you want to research will usually be near the top of the list. Click on that item and you will go straight to the Web site you want.

And if a company does not have a Web site, that tells you that the company prefers to be invisible. Why would you want to work for an invisible company? If you still want to be interviewed, a question like this probably needs to be at the top of your list:

In my research on the company, I tried to find a Web site. I did not see any reference to a Web site on the company materials, nor could I find one using any of the search engines I tried. Is this intentional, and what is the logic behind not having exposure on the Web?

Every company's Web site is different, but they are all organized in standard ways. The first thing is to look for a tab or button that says "About."

Most companies put basic background information about themselves in this area. Another area to look for is the "pressroom" or "newsroom." Many companies collect news releases and articles about themselves under this designation.

Some corporate Web sites are pretty complicated affairs, with literally tens of thousands of places to hide information. So if you are lost, most Web sites have a feature called "Site Map." This feature gives Web site visitors a high-level look at where information may be found on the site. It's like the store directory you find in a shopping mall. Finally, most Web sites have a search function. Click on the search function and type in a term such as "about" or "news releases" and let the search engine take you where you need to go.

For public companies, the annual report is almost always available at the Web site. This document is an invaluable source of information about the company and its challenges. Pay careful attention to the letter from the management. In that letter, the organization's CEO lays out the company's accomplishments and challenges. It will give you important clues for questions you can ask. In some cases, there is a Q&A format, so many of the questions you might want to ask in your interview are already there.

"The best questions to ask interviewers are those that demonstrate a knowledge of the company and its market," says Incentive Systems' Bob Conlin. "I'm always impressed by good questions about specific competitors, where the market is going in terms of trends, and how the company is adapting to those trends."

OTHER WEB RESOURCES

While a company's Web site is chock-full of information, it is not comprehensive. Few company Web sites include information that is truly critical of the company. For more objective information about the company, there are hundreds of free resources you can consult. It is beyond the scope of this book to discuss online corporate research strategies, but the following resources are what I use when I want to research a company:

CEO EXPRESS
www.ceoexpress.com
A great portal site to start your search, with links to dozens of publications

HOOVER'S, INC.
www.hoovers.com

Business information you can use on virtually every company in the United States

COMPANY SLEUTH
www.companysleuth.com

Business intelligence for investors

BUSINESS WIRE
www.businesswire.com

News releases as they are issued

SECURITIES AND EXCHANGE COMMISSION
www.sec.gov

For public companies, all the financial information you need

FUCKED COMPANY
www.fuckedcompany.com

If you want rumors, bad news, and trash about a company

BUSINESS PERIODICALS

Look at what the leading business magazines have to say about the company. A good place to start is the Web site portal CEO Express (*www.ceoexpress.com*). From this site, you can launch to dozens of specific publications and information resources, or you can do a search across all the sites it aggregates. Other good resources include:

BUSINESS WEEK
www.businessweek.com

FORTUNE
www.fortune.com

FORBES
www.forbes.com

INC.
www.inc.com

Most business journals periodically make lists of the best employers. *Fortune* magazine has its "Most Admired Corporations" issue and lists the best places to work, generally in its January and February issues. *Working Woman* publishes a list of the companies most sensitive to women professionals. *Business Week* lists the best-performing companies in America (usually in the last issue in March). Technical publications such as *ComputerWorld* (*www.computerworld.com*) and *InfoWorld* (*www.infoworld.com*) publish similar evaluations of the best high-technology companies to work for.

LOCAL NEWSPAPERS AND OTHER NEWSPAPERS

If the newspaper in the company's hometown has a business section, you will usually find good coverage of the company. Fortunately, most newspapers these days are online. So find the newspaper's Web site and search for the company you want to research. While you are at it, check out what the *New York Times* (*www.newyorktimes.com*), *Washington Post* (*www.washingtonpost.com*), and *Chicago Tribune* (*www.chicagotribune.com*) have to say about the company. For high-tech companies, I also check the *San Jose Mercury News* (*www.mercurycenter.com/*).

LOCAL BUSINESS JOURNALS

Most large metropolitan areas also have business periodicals focused on local business companies and activities. CEO Express has a link to some of the major business journal publishers including *Crain's New York* (*www.crainsny.com*) and *Crain's Chicago* (*www.crainschicagobusiness.com*). For more information, search for business journals in the community of the company you want to research.

TRADE PUBLICATIONS

There is no industry so obscure that it does not have at least one trade publication reporting on the products, people, and other developments within the industry. These publications offer the deepest information about the company and the industry in which it operates. These publications provide much more focus and detail than general business publications. In the past, trade publications were often difficult to obtain. But now many of them are online, making it much easier than ever to retrieve very focused articles on the company you are interested in

TRADE ASSOCIATIONS

America is a nation of joiners. It seems that every activity has formed an association to promote its interests. These associations exist in large part to educate the public about the good works of the members of the association. You are member of the public, so don't be shy about asking for help. Many associations now have Web sites, and the depth of their resources can be stunning. A powerful reference, found in most libraries, is the *Encyclopedia of Associations*, a directory of associations with contact information. Some associations require membership to access specific resources, but even then a nice letter to the executive director can often get you privileges to surf the site without cost.

WHAT INFORMATION SHOULD I COLLECT?

Before going into a job interview, a well-prepared candidate will have the following information about the organization:

Full name of company
Contact Information
    Mailing address
    Telephone numbers, central, and general fax number
    Web site
    General email address

Brief description of business (25 words or so)

Public or private
Year established
Revenues or sales
Rank on *Fortune* 1000 (if applicable)
Number of employees

Recent stock price (if public)
   Stock price, 52 week high
   Stock price, 52 week low
Name of chief executive officer

Chief products or services
Chief competitor
Company advantages
Company challenges

CHAPTER 5

DO YOU MIND
IF I TAKE NOTES?

WHY TAKING NOTES IS CRITICAL

Should I take notes during my job interviews?

This controversial question is far from settled, but the majority of career coaches and recruiters I talked to give you a green light to take notes during job interviews. Yes, some interviewers get nervous when a job candidate whips out a notebook and starts taking notes. But others are impressed by the professionalism and interest demonstrated by a candidate taking notes. So what should you do?

Let's look at both sides of this important question and then consider the arguments of a cross section of human resources professionals. Let's start with the naysayers.

THE ARGUMENTS AGAINST TAKING NOTES

Some job coaches believe that in American society, it is not considered appropriate to take notes during an employment interview. There are three facets to this argument.

First, when you are in conversation with someone, it is polite to pay attention to that person. Taking notes, to these coaches, is impolite.

49

Second, some job coaches trot out the argument that taking notes makes interviewers defensive, as if you are collecting evidence for a potential lawsuit. The last thing a job candidate wants to do is make the interviewer nervous.

Third, these critics suggest that if a candidate whips out a set of notes during an interview, the recruiter might conclude that the candidate has a problem with short-term memory or with thinking on his or her feet.

"I coach my candidates not to take notes during the interview because if you are taking notes you can't listen with complete attention," says Robin Upton, a career coach with Bernard Haldane Associates in Dallas, Texas. One downside, she adds, is that note taking exacerbates the natural human condition of self-deception. "We often hear a question the way we want to hear it instead of the way the interviewer actually asked it," Upton says. Candidates risk appearing evasive if they don't respond to the question that's on the table.

When he is considering applicants for senior management positions, Tom Thrower, general manager of Management Recruiters, a recruiting firm in Oakland, California, prefers candidates who display total professional self-assurance. To Thrower, note taking detracts from an expression of overwhelming organizational confidence. "I'm interested in people with good memories," he says. "I find it distracting watching applicants take notes."

The situation, Thrower concedes, is different for people applying for technical positions, such as systems analysts, or financial types such as controllers or budget officers. He expects people applying for these positions to be very detail-oriented—thus it is appropriate and encouraging to see technicians taking notes during the job interview.

THE ARGUMENTS FOR TAKING NOTES

Most job coaches and recruiters favor note taking. They believe the very real upsides outweigh the potential downsides. The fact is, most interviewers take notes themselves.

"I'm hugely okay with note takers as long as it doesn't delay our process," says Seattlejobs.org's president Janice Brookshier. "After all, I'm going to be taking notes." A job interview is not a social occasion. It is a business meeting. And in American business culture, taking notes in support of a business meeting is considered not only appropriate, but often a sign of professionalism.

Far from a sign of disorganization or weakness, taking notes is a mark of a well-organized professional. The cultures of companies such as IBM, Cisco Systems, and Computer Associates International actually encourage note taking at all meetings. Employees are issued notebooks, and they are expected to use them as part of a culture that insists that people stay accountable for the goals and objectives they take on.

Melanie Mays, a recruiter with Empyrean Consulting, Inc., in Dallas, Texas, supports note taking because it encourages candidates to listen rather than talk. "I coach candidates to apply the 80-20 rule in job interviews: You should be listening 80 percent of the time and talking only 20 percent of the time. If taking notes helps, I'm all for it."

These recruiters believe that taking notes actually keeps the attention on the speaker by minimizing interruptions as the applicant makes a list of insights and responses that can be referred to when it's the listener's turn to speak. Note taking does not have to be distracting. The point of notes is not to take down a conversation verbatim, which would be intrusive. The purpose is to remind yourself of important points that are being made and questions or comments you don't want to forget when it's your turn to talk.

The most important thing is to ask permission. "I never have a problem with people who ask permission to take notes during an interview," says Sandra Grabczynski, director of employer development at Career-Site.com, an online recruiting service in Ann Arbor, Michigan. "It generally impresses me that the applicant is taking the opportunity seriously." Whipping out a notebook without asking permission may strike some interviewers as presumptuous.

Candidates are not the only ones taking notes. Rich Franklin, HR director at KnowledgePoint, a software maker in Petaluma, California, prefaces most interviews by saying that he will be making a few notes during the course of the interview. "At that point, I invite them to take notes as well, if they want," Franklin says, adding that he's gratified when they do. "Benefits and insurance plans can be pretty complicated, so I appreciate candidates taking notes. It shows me they are serious."

THE RULES OF THE GAME

Ask Permission

Asking permission is a simple thing, but it makes a big difference. First, it's respectful. Second, it draws attention to the behavior, so that the interviewer is not surprised. Surprises are rarely in the candidate's favor. Here are some suggested wordings for getting permission:

Do you mind if I take notes? I want to keep the details of this discussion very clear in my mind because the more I learn about this opportunity, the more confident I am that I can make an important contribution.

Notice how the applicant embeds a selling message in her request.

Also ask permission before you look at your notes when you ask your questions:

While we were talking, I jotted down a few points I wanted to ask about. May I have a minute to consult my notes?

Or:

Thanks for the detailed description of the opportunity and the company. I know you answered most of my questions in the course of our conversation. Before I came here, I jotted down a few questions I didn't want to forget. May I consult my notes?

USE A NOTEBOOK

In Chapter 1, I suggested ordering questions by writing them on index cards. That's a useful practice as you determine which questions to ask and in which order to ask them. But after you have established the questions and their order, transfer the list to a handsome leather-bound notebook. Whipping out a set of index cards sends the wrong message. Plus there's always the risk of the index cards slipping out of your hand and flying all over the place.

One of the reasons for having a notebook in the interview is that you will think of questions to ask the interviewer. Perhaps the interviewer is talking about a new product that the company is about to launch. You remember in your previous job how one of the product launches hit an unexpected snag and how you helped unravel the problem. You don't want to interrupt the interviewer, so you make a quick note to talk about the incident later in the interview.

"Remember, first impressions are critical," says CareerSite.com's Grabczynski. "If you're going to take notes, don't use a pencil or loose scraps of paper or the back of your parking ticket. Use a fine pen and a clean, professional notebook, preferably bound in leather." The pen you select makes a statement about you. Make sure it reflects the professional you. A fountain pen is good if you know how you use it. A little silver one might be fine, but not gold. And for pity's sake, make sure it works. Nothing will defeat your purpose more than you fumbling with a pen that runs out of ink. Asking the job interviewer for a pen is something you definitely want to avoid. And as long as we're on writing utensils, now's not the time to pull a chewed pencil out from behind your ear. If you're applying to be an art director, you can maybe get away with using a colored marker, but otherwise the interviewer will wonder if you can be trusted with sharp objects.

BODY LANGUAGE

Make sure your body language remains open. That means keeping the pad on the table instead of on your lap. Learn how to take notes while still maintaining occasional eye contact. "Don't let your note taking close you off from the interviewer," Mays says. "If you can't take notes without interfering with open body language, don't take notes."

At the same time, keep your note taking discreet. You don't want to give the impression that you're a detective and your note taking might be used against the interviewer. You know you have crossed the line when the interviewer asks if you're going to read him his Miranda rights before questioning.

Learn to take notes without losing eye contact. Interviewers will be insulted if all they have to talk to is the top of your head. Taking notes while keeping your head up is a skill that must be practiced. Here's one way to practice this important skill: Turn on the TV to one of the Sunday interview programs. As you take notes on the interviewer's questions, practice keeping your eyes on the screen, glancing down only occasionally. You'll know you're ready for prime time when you can record the questions in shorthand and are able to repeat the questions.

WAIT FOR THE INTERVIEWER TO SPEAK

The most important thing to remember is that you should take notes only when the interviewer is speaking. You should never take notes or even refer to them when you are answering questions. Interviewers want to see how you think on your feet, not how you read notes. The one exception, as mentioned earlier, is that when the interviewer asks if you have questions, you can ask permission to refer to your notes.

Always be prepared with at least four questions created specifically for each interview. These questions should be carefully crafted to reflect the basic research you have done on the company combined with the strongest aspects of your experience and qualifications. Then, if the interviewer surprises you with "Do you have any questions at this point?" you will be ready to go without fumbling.

Finally, if you are still not sure whether going into an interview with a notebook is an advantage or not, consider this comment from John Hawke, CEO of Howe Barnes Investments, a Chicago brokerage company specializing in community and regional banks. Here he is discussing motivation: "When you want people to move to the next level of performance, go to them with a notebook in hand. Get them to step outside themselves."

There's that comment: "Go to them with a notebook in hand." If you go with empty hands, it indicates that you don't intend to hear anything worth saving, that you've gone into the meeting with your mind made up, rather than to work together to arrive at a decision. Maybe I'm making too much of it, but I believe that going into any group process with a notebook in hand signals that you respect the contributions of the other members in the process and are ready to attend to what they say with your whole being. "Empty hands, closed minds," visualizes Dale Dauten, a syndicated business columnist based in Phoenix, Arizona, who writes under the title "Corporate Curmudgeon."

WHAT ABOUT ELECTRONIC DEVICES?

What about electronic devices such as Palm Pilots, other personal digital assistants (PDAs), and notebook computers? Should you bring them with you into the interviewing room?

More and more people are. In our increasingly wired society, paper notebooks and even Daytimer organizers are yielding to electronic devices, so it is natural that more of them are showing up at job interviews. And they are not all brought in by candidates. Many companies issue their HR people Palm Pilots or similar devices. "If you are thoughtful and appropriate, a PDA will not seem out of place in a job interview," says Handspring's Beau Harris. "The important thing is not to become so focused on the technology that it keeps the interviewer from getting to know you."

Mountain View, California–based Handspring markets the popular Visor line of PDAs, so it is not surprising that Harris is impressed when a job candidate whips out a Visor during the course of the interview. Of course, candidates have a sheepish grin when they pull out a Palm Pilot or other competitor. "Don't worry," Harris tells them. "If you get the job, we'll get you a Visor." Harris uses his Visor throughout the interview. If time is an issue, the Visor will silently vibrate, alerting Harris that the interview should come to a close. If he wants to bring the candidate in for a second interview, Harris has his calendar right in front of him. If the candidate also has a PDA, it becomes very easy to set up the next meeting.

KnowledgePoint's Rich Franklin is especially impressed when candidates pull out a PDA. "These folks definitely get a plus for organization," he continues. "I really appreciate it when I want to set up a second interview. Candidates with PDAs can check their schedules on the spot, instead of having to get back to me."

Handspring's Harris has observed how powerfully candidates can use their PDAs to streamline the interview process. "Filling out job applications becomes much easier when they have their address book and calendar with them," he says. Harris has often bonded with candidates around applications on their Visors. Occasionally, candidate and recruiter will even share cool applications by beaming them back and forth.

"Every job these days involves creating something on computers," says Liz Reiersen, a senior technical recruiter at Verizon Communications in Irving, Texas. "Notebook computers are great for people to demonstrate computer code, spreadsheets, or marketing materials they developed."

But some companies may still be leery about electronic devices other than personal organizers being brought in and out of the office. Organizations that do secret work for the military and have intense security practices may have policies about bringing in electronics. In any case, it might delay you in getting in and out of the building. Check in advance if you want to bring anything more substantial than a notebook computer into one of these companies.

Finally, a note about using audiotape recorders: Don't. A tape reorder will make interviewers nervous and cautious, the last thing you want them to be. With everyone so sensitive to litigation, don't give them any excuse to wonder how you might use the tape against them. Tape recorders set up a vibe that either you don't trust your memory or you don't trust the interviewer. It's bad news either way.

PART II

INTERVIEW THE INTERVIEWER

All interviews are important, but some are more important than others.

The one interview that is all important is with the person who has the final hiring authority. We'll call that person the hiring manager.

All other job interviews, while important, have the agenda of screening you out. When you meet with recruiters or human resources, you are being evaluated for whether you are a good enough fit to have an interview with the only person with the authority to offer you a job. Thus your strategy for presenting yourself and the questions you ask depends on whom you are interviewed by. There are three general classes of interviewers:

- Recruiter or headhunter
- Human resources
- Hiring manager

In Part II, we will look at the different expectations and roles of each of these types. Because the expectations and the power of each of these groups within the organization differ, the questions you ask will necessarily be different. You don't want to ask a hiring manager detailed questions about health benefits. By the same token, recruiters probably don't know intimate details about the specific tools or programs you will use in your job. So don't waste precious time on questions they can't answer. In the next three chapters you will find the best questions appropriate to each category of interviewers. These are the questions that will promote your application and maximize the opportunity for you to advance to the next level.

Because your interview with the hiring manager, the only person with the authority to give you a job, is the most important, most of the best questions are concentrated in Chapter 8.

Note: Because every interview situation is different, it is critical that you personalize each question to the requirements of the particular interview. Consider the phrasings of the questions in this book as jumping-off points for you to personalize questions for your job interviews. To reinforce this point, the book offers variations for asking questions in different ways. The more you customize your questions for the demands of each interview, the more authentic you will appear.

CHAPTER 6

QUESTIONS FOR HEADHUNTERS, RECRUITERS, AND STAFFING AGENCIES

IMPORTANT INTERMEDIARIES IN YOUR JOB SEARCH

Headhunters and recruiters can be your best friends during your job search. They can present you to dozens of employers. They can coach you on your résumé and interview skills. And frequently they can get the kind of feedback that employers rarely entrust to individual candidates.

But remember that recruiters can't hire you. They are intermediaries who add value to their clients by screening and presenting qualified job candidates. Occasionally their endorsement carries significant weight. If they recommend you highly, it increases your chances of getting a job. But recruiters can't make you an offer. Only their clients (called "principals") can do that.

CONTINGENCY AND RETAINER AGENCIES

There are two types of recruiting agencies: contingency and retainer. Some agencies do both. But in general, contingency agencies are paid

Memorably Good Question
#1

What's the makeup of the team as far as experience? Am I going to be a mentor, or will I be mentored?

This question shows that the candidate is sensitive to where he will fit in the organization relative to the skill level of the other members of the team. It also demonstrates a willingness to teach or be taught, in either case evidence of a team player.

Houston Landry
Avalanche Communications Group
Dallas, TX

Memorably Bad Question
#1

Can I switch jobs with the hiring manager?

The candidate looked at the job in question but wanted the hiring manager's job because it was a better position. He thought it would be "really easy" for the hiring manager to take the candidate's existing job, creating a better opportunity for the candidate. I thought the candidate was kidding, but he wasn't. I warned him that if he contacted the hiring manager, it would critically reduce his chances of getting the job he was interviewing for, but he didn't listen. The hiring manager thought this guy must have eaten paint chips as a kid. Needless to say, he did not get the job.

Jason Rodd
Senior Consultant
TMP Worldwide, Inc.
Tampa, FL

only if they present a candidate who accepts a position. Retainer agencies are paid whether they present a candidate or not, but they look a hell of a lot better if they present qualified candidates.

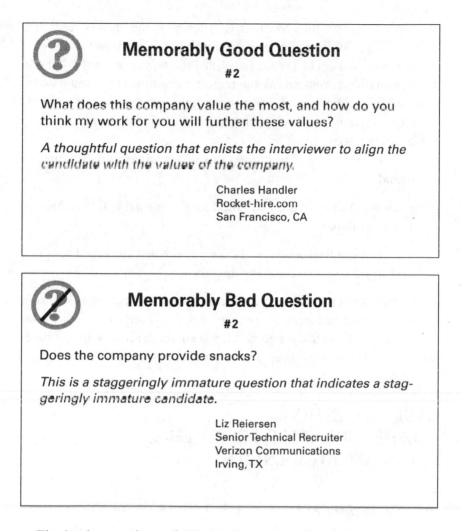

Memorably Good Question

#2

What does this company value the most, and how do you think my work for you will further these values?

A thoughtful question that enlists the interviewer to align the candidate with the values of the company.

Charles Handler
Rocket-hire.com
San Francisco, CA

Memorably Bad Question

#2

Does the company provide snacks?

This is a staggeringly immature question that indicates a staggeringly immature candidate.

Liz Reiersen
Senior Technical Recruiter
Verizon Communications
Irving, TX

That's why recruiters of either stripe want to like you, or at least believe you can do the job. They want to be able to refer you to their clients. They want their clients to agree that you are as qualified as they believe you are. They don't get paid unless three conditions are met: One, their client agrees and offers you a job; two, you accept the job; and three, you are successful on the job—or at least stay with the job for a specified period of time, generally three months to a year. So if you are at all qualified, they are going to do everything within reason to sell you on the company and sell the company on you.

Your interview with a recruiter is different in tone and content than with an employer. In some cases, you will not even know the name of the company the agency represents until the recruiter is satisfied that you are qualified. You can ask the recruiter questions that would be inappropriate to ask the employer. For example, questions about compensation that you would not initiate with the employer are perfectly reasonable to ask a recruiter.

So your strategy in asking questions of recruiters and headhunters is twofold:

- Demonstrate that you are qualified for the job and will likely take it if it is offered to you.

- Get critical information about the company that you might not be able to get from the company directly.

Another good thing about recruiters is that they represent dozens or sometimes even hundreds of companies. Even if one opportunity does not work out, if you make a good impression on a recruiter, the recruiter will remember you and keep you in mind for other searches he or she may have.

25 BEST QUESTIONS
FOR HEADHUNTERS, RECRUITERS,
AND STAFFING AGENCIES

6-1
How did you find me?
Headhunters hate this question, but ask it anyway, because the answer will tell you which resources (job sites, networking, placement services) are producing results for you in your search for a more rewarding opportunity.

6-2
Is this a retainer or contingency assignment?
This will give you a clue about the relationship between the recruiter and the principal. Generally, agencies on retainer have a closer relationship with the principal, and their endorsement carries a lot more clout.

Memorably Good Question

#3

What kinds of processes are in place to help me work collaboratively?

This candidate shows me not only that he wants to succeed, but that he understands that success at this level requires a collaborative effort.

Bob Conlin
VP of Marketing
Incentive Systems
Bedford, MA

6-3

Are you dealing with the client's HR people, or do you have direct contact with the hiring manager?

Don't be afraid to ask. You want to know how much influence the recruiter will have with this client. A search engagement that puts the recruiter in direct contact with the hiring manager will offer a significantly stronger opportunity for you to be placed in the position.

6-4

How long has the client been with you?

This gives you insight into how well the recruiter knows the company. Look for a long-term association.

6-5

How many candidates have you personally placed with this client?

Look for a recruiter that has a successful history with the client, better yet, with the hiring manager. The recruiter should have a solid understanding of the client's needs in order to determine if you will fit into the position, the work team, and the corporate culture. If the recruiter has not placed any candidates with the company, there is a chance that he or she really does not have a specific assignment or position in mind for you. What the recruiter is doing is trolling for candidates to add to his or her database for future engagements.

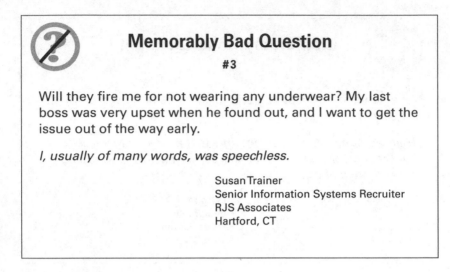

Memorably Bad Question

#3

Will they fire me for not wearing any underwear? My last boss was very upset when he found out, and I want to get the issue out of the way early.

I, usually of many words, was speechless.

Susan Trainer
Senior Information Systems Recruiter
RJS Associates
Hartford, CT

6-6

Tell me about your career choice. How did you get into recruiting?

Just as the recruiter is screening you, let the recruiter know you are screening him or her. Learn more about his or her skill level and experience as a recruiter. If the recruiter has less than two years of experience, he or she is still in the process of learning the trade.

6-7

When will I find out the name of the principal or client company?

A relationship between a recruiter and a candidate should be built on a foundation of trust, honesty, and respect. Most recruiters will provide client information to you right after they have presented your résumé to the client. If the recruiter will not agree to these terms, you should question the recruiter's reasons for withholding the information and decide if you want this person to represent you.

6-8

May I have a written job description?

It probably doesn't exist, and if it does, you probably won't get it; but it pays to ask. If you get something, it will have important information about required skills, responsibilities, and perhaps even the compensation package. At the minimum, you need to know the title and level of the position.

6-9
Where is the position located?
You want to determine if this opportunity matches your geographic requirements.

6-10
Where is the company headquartered?
You want to know if you will be working at headquarters or at a regional branch. If the latter, you will want to know if working at a remote location represents a liability to your visibility and prospects for advancement.

6-11
To whom does the position report?
You want to know the name or at least the title of the person you will be working for.

6-12
Can you tell me about this executive's management style?
You want to get as much information about the supervisor as possible.

6-13
Why is the position open?
You want to know the circumstances of the position. Is it a new position? If not, what happened to the last person in the job? Did he or she quit, and if so, why? Was he or she promoted?

 Memorably Bad Question
#4

I need to leave the interview for a minute. Do you have a match?

Yes, your application for employment and the circular file. An applicant for a branch manager's position asked to leave for a cigarette break in the middle of the interview, and then came back a few seconds later to offer this remarkable question.

ACT-1 Recruiter
Raleigh, NC

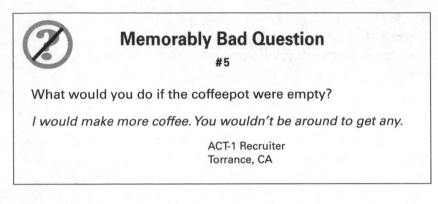

Memorably Bad Question

#5

What would you do if the coffeepot were empty?

I would make more coffee. You wouldn't be around to get any.

ACT-1 Recruiter
Torrance, CA

6-14
What happened to the person who previously held this position?
Look for indications that the incumbent was promoted within the organization.

6-15
Is this a new position?
A new position indicates the company is growing.

6-16
How long has the position been open?
This gives you a clue about your chances and the desirability of the position. If the position has been open more than three months, something is not right. You need to find out what it is about the position or company that makes the position hard to fill.

6-17
How long have you been working on the assignment?
Again, if the recruiter has been trying to fill the position for three months or more, something is suspicious. You need to find out what.

6-18
What does the position pay?
While bringing up pay and compensation before the interviewer does is a no-no when you are interviewing with human resources or the hiring manager, here it is perfectly acceptable. There is no point in wasting each other's time if your requirements and the position's pay structure are wildly divergent.

6-19

Are there any pay or compensation constraints that I should take into consideration?

This question allows the recruiter to talk about any ceilings or limits on salary that the position imposes. Some recruiters are instructed not to present candidates who demand more than the preset salary. If that's the case, you want to know it.

6-20

What can you tell me about the person who will be interviewing me?

If the recruiter recommends you, you want to know something about the person you will interview with next.

6-21

What is his or her position, title, management style?

You want to know if the next person to interview you will be a gatekeeper or a person with actual hiring authority.

6-22

Who will make the final hiring decision?

If the answer to the question above does not give you the critical information you need, ask for it directly.

6-23

After you present my résumé, when can I expect to hear from you regarding the status of this position?

Set expectations with the recruiter about the frequency of updates regarding your candidacy. You should also insist that the recruiter inform you about other opportunities and ask for your permission before presenting you to any other clients. This tells the recruiter you are a professional.

6-24

Can you describe, specifically, how the company navigates/balances work–personal life issues?

This question will help you get some insight into what level of workaholism runs in the company.

6-25

What might I do that would violate the culture of the company during my interview?

Corporate culture is tricky to describe but putting it this way makes it easier to understand the culture and to avoid doing something to violate it.

Five Ways to Get Recruiters on Your Side

We all need all the help we can get. A trusting relationship with a professional recruiter can move your career ahead. You can do your part to establish that trust by observing the following guidelines. Remember that the employer compensates recruiters. But it's a win-win situation. They win when they refer you for a position you accept.

1. Be up front about your financial needs and goals.

2. Take time to learn about the recruiter's practice and the markets he or she serves.

3. Establish the ground rules for how you plan to work together and avoid duplication of effort.

4. Offer names of other candidates who may fit a recruiter's portfolio. In appreciation, the recruiter may set up more interviews for you.

5. Recruiters want you to be successful. Ask them to coach you for the interviews they arrange.

CHAPTER 7

QUESTIONS FOR HUMAN RESOURCES

ENABLING HR PEOPLE TO WORK FOR YOU

Human resources people can be professional, genuinely warm, and encouraging, but, at their best, HR people are gatekeepers. Their main function is to screen candidates out so that the ultimate hiring authority can select from a manageable number of candidates. HR people have no hiring authority themselves.

THE CARE AND FEEDING OF HR PEOPLE

Your job search will likely include working with HR screeners, so you should know a few things about their care and feeding. If you keep their agenda in mind, play it straight, and make it easy for them to do their jobs, you will be able to advance your application to the hiring authority. The questions in this chapter are designed to give the HR screener maximum confidence that he or she will not regret endorsing your application.

The central truism about HR people is that, as a profession, they are highly risk-averse. A nightmare for HR people is that the candidate they endorsed will melt down in the next interview or, worse, be hired and then turn out to be a lemon. When that happens, guess who gets clobbered? Right. The poor HR screener who missed the candidate's signs of pathology that, in retrospect, were as glaring as a Times Square billboard. The result? If an HR screener has the slightest hesitation about you or your interview, she (HR screeners are overwhelmingly women) will simply go on to the next candidate. Given the economy and the large number of qualified candidates competing for each position these days, HR people won't hesitate to move on if you give them any reason to question your desirability as a candidate.

So your first strategy is to not give them any doubt about your application. To do that you must be immediately interested, positive, and likable. Confidence is important, but avoid cockiness. Remember, your starting salary will always be higher—sometimes dramatically higher—than the salary of the interviewer. Don't give the interviewer another excuse to dislike you.

ALLY WITH THE HR INTERVIEWER

Your second strategy is to win the HR interviewer as an ally. If you treat the HR interviewer as an impediment rather than as a person, you convey arrogance and rudeness. Your attitude also raises questions about your ability to work with every person on the team. So in the interview, you will make yourself look attractive by genuinely caring about the HR person's opinion. Listen thoughtfully and gratefully. Treat the HR person with respect, knowing HR's contributions as well as HR's limitations in the decision-making process. Don't lay it on too thick, but if you do it well, the HR person will tend to move your application to the thin pile that says "maybe" instead of the thick pile marked "no way."

In other words, your strategy in interviewing with HR is to satisfy your interviewer that if he or she passes your file to the hiring manager and you subsequently get the job, there will be no possibility that you will embarrass him or her. To do that, you need to persuade the HR person of three things:

- That you are qualified to do the job
- That you want to do the job
- That if given the job, you will fit in

Memorably Good Question

#4

What attracted you to this company, and what do you think are its strengths and weaknesses?

The question flatters the interviewer and creates a personal connection. If you create a bond with the interviewer, you're going to get better, more authentic information on which to base a decision.

Jeanette Grill
Director of Professional Experience and
    Placement
Long Island University, CW Post Campus
Brookville, NY

If you do, your application will move to where you want it to be: in front of the hiring manager, the only one in the organization with the power to give you the job you want.

Many HR people are informed, empathic, and professional, and they want you to succeed. Most of them are willing to assist you in refining your résumé, cover letter, or interviewing techniques. Many of them have gone out of their way to help me with this book. If you are fortunate enough to get one of these folks on your side, they can really make the interviewing process much more productive and enjoyable.

HR people need to be respected, says Joel Hamroff, president of Magill Associates, Inc., a staffing service in Levittown, New York. "Remember that the person sitting on the other side of the desk at one time sat where you are sitting and they are at least as smart as you are. Human resources folks need a reason to exist, so the more you can ask about their experiences and opinions, the more it will endear you to them."

But the bottom line remains: HR people cannot give you the job you want. Nor can they give you the facts-on-the-ground important information you need to make a good career decision. For the most part, HR people are well informed in a general sense about the company and its benefits policies. But they probably don't have a lot of the specific information you want about the position and the people you will be working with.

30 BEST QUESTIONS FOR HUMAN RESOURCES

7-1
Why do you enjoy working for this company?
Go for a personal relationship right away. Show the HR person you care about his or her experience and opinion. Plus you'll get some useful information about the company and its culture.

7-2
What attracted you to this organization?
Everybody likes to talk about themselves. Maybe the HR person will tell you a story about how he or she got there. That means that person trusts you.

7-3
Can you describe the work environment here?
This is another way of asking about how the company works.

7-4
How do you describe the philosophy of the company or organization?
It's great to ask the HR interviewer's perspective on this point.

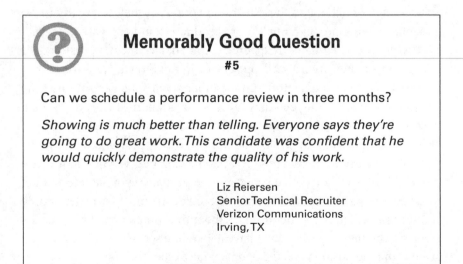

? **Memorably Good Question**

#5

Can we schedule a performance review in three months?

Showing is much better than telling. Everyone says they're going to do great work. This candidate was confident that he would quickly demonstrate the quality of his work.

Liz Reiersen
Senior Technical Recruiter
Verizon Communications
Irving, TX

Memorably Bad Question
#6

If I don't take a lunch break, can I accumulate the time that I am forgoing and add it to my vacation time?

This candidate is already out to lunch. This question displays a fatal lack of judgment because the answer is so predictable. There is not a company in the world that would agree to such a business. As a general rule, any question with the word "lunch" in it is inappropriate.

Richard Kathnelson
VP of Human Resources
Syndesis, Inc.
Ontario, Canada

7-5

What do you consider to be the organization's strengths and weaknesses?
Again, it's the interviewer's opinion that is at the heart of the question.

7-6

Can you tell me more about my day-to-day responsibilities?
Listen for items that are emphasized or repeated. These are the hot buttons, and you will want to tailor the discussion of your skills relating to these areas.

7-7

How soon are you looking to fill this position?
Get a sense of the company's time frame.

7-8

How do my skills compare with those of the other candidates you have interviewed?
It's worth a shot to ask, although you probably won't get a straight answer. Be prepared for the counter, "Why do you ask?"

7-9

I have really enjoyed meeting with you and your team, and I am very interested in the opportunity. I feel my skills and experience would be a good match for this position. What is the next step in your interview process?

This is a very strong concluding question to an interview with HR. It expresses interest, reinforces confidence, and puts the ball into the interviewer's court.

7-10

Before I leave, is there anything else you need to know concerning my ability to do this job?

This is another positive way to end the interview, emphasizing your commitment to action.

7-11

In your opinion, what is the most important contribution that this company expects from its employees?

Notice how the question solicits the interviewer's opinion.

7-12

Is there a structured career path at the company?

Some large companies and government agencies have career ladders, grade levels, and other formal steps for people to advance.

7-13

What are my prospects for advancement? If I do a good job, what is a logical next step?

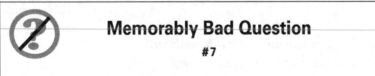

Memorably Bad Question

#7

So what is it exactly that you guys do?

If you don't know and couldn't be bothered to find out, it tells me you have no right to be in this culture where people are proud of what they do here.

Beau Harris
Recruiter
Handspring, Inc.
Mountain View, CA

Memorably Bad Question

#8

Are there any apartment complexes nearby that offer a fitness center and free wine and cheese tasting?

This sounded an alarm, because my experience is that unusual requests like this right from the beginning always lead to requests that my clients can't fulfill in the end.

Jason Rodd
Senior Consultant
TMP Worldwide, Inc.
Tampa, FL

Some companies have more or less formal career progressions—for example, programmer to systems analyst to team leader to project manager to project director, in that order.

7-14

Assuming I was hired and performed well for a period of time, what additional opportunities might this job lead to?

This tells the interviewer that you are looking past this assignment, that you are thinking of sticking around. HR people like that, because it makes them look good when one of their hires stays for a while.

7-15

Do the most successful people in the company tend to come from one area of the company, such as sales or engineering, or do they rise from a cross section of functional areas?

This question immediately tells the interviewer you are sophisticated. The culture of most companies invariably favors employees from one department or another. Technology companies frequently favor employees from engineering. The CEOs of financial companies frequently come out of finance. Most industrial CEOs come out of sales. Perhaps the interviewer will go through the five most senior officers of the company with respect to their origins. Your goal is to note whether the department you plan to join is one of the favored developing grounds for the corner offices.

Memorably Bad Question
#9

Why do I have to fill out this job application? It's all on my résumé.

Treat the job application as your first assignment for the company. Who needs someone who resists work even before they are hired?

Melanie Mays
Empyrean Consulting
Dallas, TX

7-16
I know that for the position for which I am interviewing, the company has decided to recruit from outside the organization. How do you decide between recruiting from within and going outside?

This question lets the interviewer talk about the relative merits of promoting from within and bringing in new ideas and talent (hopefully yours!) to meet the needs of the company. A good answer is that the company is growing too fast for internal promotions to support its challenges.

7-17
How does this position relate to the bottom line?

This is an inquiry into the significance of the job or department. If the job has only an indirect impact on the bottom line, when times get tough it can be considered an expense center rather than a profit center.

7-18
What advice would you give to someone in my position?

Don't lay it on too thick, but this kind of question can make an HR person's day.

7-19
How did you get into your profession?

Remember, "profession," not "job."

7-20

What major problems are we facing right now in this department or position?

Note the use of the inclusive "we."

7-21

Can you give me a formal, written description of the position? I'm interested in reviewing in detail the major activities involved and what results are expected.

This is a good question to pose to the screen interviewer. It will help you prepare to face the hiring manager.

7-22

Does this job usually lead to other positions in the company? Which ones?

You don't want to find yourself in a dead-end job. But also be sure you don't give the impression that you want to get out of the job before you are in it. Remember, the HR manager wants to see stability tempered by "long-termism."

7-23

Can you please tell me a little bit about the people with whom I'll be working most closely?

What a powerful question for finding out about your team!

 Memorably Bad Question

#10

What's the story with the receptionist?

The candidate was referring to a very attractive receptionist at the company. Who wants the risk of a harassment case? Next!

Bob Conlin
VP of Marketing
Incentive Systems
Bedford, MA

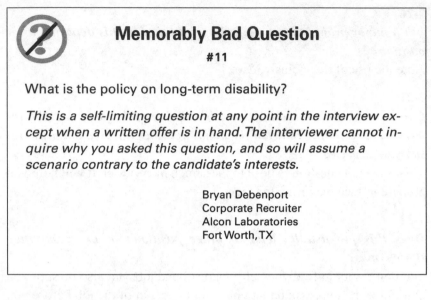

Memorably Bad Question

#11

What is the policy on long-term disability?

This is a self-limiting question at any point in the interview except when a written offer is in hand. The interviewer cannot inquire why you asked this question, and so will assume a scenario contrary to the candidate's interests.

Bryan Debenport
Corporate Recruiter
Alcon Laboratories
Fort Worth, TX

7-24

As I understand the position, the title is _____, the duties are _____, and the department is called _____. I would report directly to _____. Is that right?

This is an exercise in getting to "yes" plus demonstrating that you have command of the facts.

7-25

Can you talk about the company's commitment to equal opportunity and diversity?

Possible follow-up questions include, What's the percentage of women or minorities in the executive ranks? Does the company have a diversity officer?

7-26

Who are the company's stars, and how was their status determined?

This indicates you want to be a star, as well.

7-27

How are executives addressed by their subordinates?

You are asking about the formality of the organization.

7-28

What can you tell me about the prevailing management style?

This is an inquiry into the management style favored by the senior executives.

7-29

If you hired me, what would be my first assignment?

Message: Setting priorities and goals is key to you.

7-30

Does the company have a mission statement? May I see it?

Mission statements are an important reflection of an organization's culture. To be fair, they are generally meaningless, but the fact that the company went to the trouble to formulate one is a positive sign, and asking for it makes you look thoughtful and introspective. Be careful, though. Don't ask for a mission statement if it is posted on the company's Web site. That would make you look lazy.

CHAPTER 8

QUESTIONS FOR HIRING MANAGERS

THE ONLY PARTY THAT CAN GIVE YOU WHAT YOU WANT

Every interview is a conversation. It starts with small talk and then progresses from the general to the specific, from the abstract to the concrete. In general, the further into the interview you are, the easier it is to ask questions and the more probing your questions may appropriately become.

If you want a job, the important thing is to have a conversation with someone who has the authority to give you one.

THE HIRING MANAGER NEEDS YOU

You are aware of the pressure you are under to get a job. But the hiring manager is probably under greater pressure to hire someone than you're aware of. In fact, the only reason hiring managers take time out of their impossibly busy schedules is because important tasks are going unattended. They have work that must be done and no one with the required experience to do it. Until they hire the right person, the optimum performance of their teams is being compromised. Their bonuses, indeed their very jobs, may well be on the line. Don't forget, hiring managers have to answer to their managers, and their ability to keep their department staffed at full level is a big piece of their compensation. A good perspective to take is that you are essential for their success.

Remember, most hiring managers aren't skilled interviewers. They have little or no training in this area, and that lack of training will frequently show. If they seem nervous, ask you inappropriate questions, or are rude, try not to take it personally.

Most hiring managers don't like interviewing. They regard it as an intrusion on their precious time that prevents them from attending to their primary responsibilities. In addition, they don't like to say no. As a result, they generally don't prepare very well and are often nervous. The more you can set hiring managers at ease and persuade them that you can start making their lives easier, the better your chances.

35 BEST QUESTIONS FOR HIRING MANAGERS

8-1
What specific skills from the person you hire would make your life easier?
This question focuses the conversation squarely on the proposition that the employer has a problem. As the potential new hire, you want the employer to tell you that you can make his or her life easier because your skills are just the ticket.

 Memorably Good Question

#6

What are the most critical factors for success in your segment of the business?

Notice if the interviewer mentions people.

Kim Rutherford
Regional Vice President
Drake Beam Morin
New York, NY

8-2

What are some of the problems that keep you up at night?
This is another way to uncover the employer's hot buttons, subtly suggesting that hiring you will bring immediate relief to the interviewer's insomnia.

8-3

What would be a surprising but positive thing the new person could do in the first 90 days?
The wording here is designed to reveal the interviewer's "wish list" for what the new hire can offer.

8-4

How does upper management perceive this part of the organization?
The response to this question will give the job seeker a feel for how valuable the department is to upper management, because if and when the organization goes through a financial crisis, you want to know that your department will not be the first department cut.

8-5

What do you see as the most important opportunities for improvement in the area I hope to join?
This is another way to get some clues about what specific improvements the hiring manager desires.

8-6

What are the organization's three most important goals?
This answer will provide an important clue for you if you take the job, because you'll be evaluated on your contribution to those three goals.

8-7

How do you see this position impacting on the achievement of those goals?
This answer will give an important clue about whether the job is important. If the answer is essentially "not much," you are being considered for a nonessential position.

8-8

What attracted you to working for this organization?
Get the hiring manager to tell you a story. Listen carefully for clues about what makes for success.

8-9

What have you liked most about working here?

Shared stories are what create community. Here's another way to bond with the interviewer around a story.

8-10

In what ways has the experience surprised or disappointed you?

Follow-up is good. If the interviewer feels safe, he or she may actually share a disappointment.

8-11

What are the day-to-day responsibilities I'll be assigned?

No better way to know what you'll be doing. Notice how the question gently assumes you are already on the team.

8-12

Could you explain the company's organizational structure?

Ask this question if there is something you don't understand about the organization.

8-13

What is the organization's plan for the next five years, and how does this department or division fit in?

Any question that implies you have the long term in mind is great. The hiring manager is thinking, "This guy aims to stick around for the long term."

8-14

Will we be expanding or bringing on new products or new services that I should be aware of?

Notice the use of the word "we." This is another question that allows the hiring manager to discuss future plans and prospects.

8-15

What are some of the skills and abilities you see as necessary for someone to succeed in this job?

This is another way to uncover possible objections or conflicts. Again, you can't address an objection unless it's articulated.

Memorably Good Question

#7

What can I bring Company XYZ to round out the team?

The question suggests the reality that the team is missing some key resource. It asks the interviewer to consider how the candidate's skill set may be just what the team is missing.

Beau Harris
Recruiter
Handspring, Inc.
Mountain View, CA

8-16

What challenges might I encounter if I take on this position?

Listen carefully. The hiring manager is telling you where you are expected to fail. Is this a challenge you can take on and at which you can reasonably hope to succeed? If Superman couldn't hack it, watch out! You're being set up for failure.

8-17

What are your major concerns that need to be immediately addressed in this job?

Note the emphasis on the word "your." This is less about the organization's agenda than the hiring manager's concerns. They may or may not be different. It won't serve you well to meet the organization's goals but not your manager's.

8-18

What are the attributes of the job that you'd like to see improved?

This is another way of asking the hiring manager for the conditions of success.

8-19

What is your company's policy on attending seminars, workshops, and other training opportunities?

You want to be seen as interested in learning and gaining new skill sets. You want your organization to support those goals.

8-20
What is the budget this department operates with?
You may or may not get a straight answer to this straight question, but asking shows you understand the power of budgets to control outcomes.

8-21
What committees and task forces will I be expected to participate in?
Whether you like committee work or not, you should get this information to make an informed decision.

8-22
How will my leadership responsibilities and performance be measured? By whom?
Here's another general question that goes to how your efforts will be evaluated. It's likely you will start a conversation about metrics such as management by objective.

8-23
Are there any weaknesses in the department that you are particularly looking to improve?
This will provide an indication of what your first assignment will be.

8-24
What are the department's goals, and how do they align with the company's mission?
This is another way to get a picture of how the department fits into the enterprise.

8-25
What are the company's strengths and weaknesses compared with the competition (name one or two companies)?
This question shows that you have done your research and that you are rightfully aware that success means outperforming the competition.

8-26
How does the reporting structure work here? What are the preferred means of communication?
This set of questions goes to the heart of the corporate culture. Are reporting structures formal or informal? You will not be happy if you pre-

Memorably Good Question
#8

In what area could your team use a little polishing?

This question creates a super opportunity for the candidate to talk about experience that complements the area identified by the interviewer.

> Susan Trainer
> Senior Information Systems Recruiter
> RJS Associates
> Hartford, CT

fer an informal, open-door company environment and this company prefers a more rigid structure.

8-27
What goals or objectives need to be achieved in the next six months?
Here is another question to let the hiring manager know that you want to do one thing at a time starting with the most important thing.

8-28
Can you give me an idea of the typical day and workload and the special demands the job has?
This is a good question to get a sense of the job on a day-to-day basis.

8-29
This is a new position. What are the forces that suggested the need for this position?
As the holder of a brand-new position, you will have a lot of freedom to shape the job. But the first thing to understand is why it was created and what problem it is designed to solve.

8-30
What areas of the job would you like to see improvement in with regard to the person who was most recently performing these duties?
This should give you a clue about why the incumbent failed. Yes it's true that people can learn only from mistakes, but that doesn't mean it has

Memorably Good Question
#9

Do team members typically eat lunch together, or do they typically eat at their workstations?

This question is a great indicator of how cohesive the team is. If the candidate wants to contribute in a highly collaborative atmosphere, he will likely feel isolated in a company where people eat lunch by themselves.

> Melanie Mays
> Empyrean Consulting
> Dallas, TX

to be their own mistakes. The downside is that if the incumbent left on bad terms, you risk associating yourself with some negative vibes.

8-31
From all I can see, I'd really like to work here, and I believe I can add considerable value to the company. What's the next step in the selection process?
Express continued interest, ask for the job, and establish a time frame for the next step.

8-32
How does this position contribute to the company's goals, productivity, or profits?
This question demonstrates your acknowledgment that every position must make a direct contribution to the company's bottom line. Follow up with a commitment to doing just that.

8-33
What is currently the most pressing business issue or problem for the company or department?
This is an opportunity to get into a very useful conversation about the challenges you will be expected to face.

8-34

Would you describe for me the actions of a person who previously achieved success in this position?

This question gives the hiring manager an opportunity to reflect on his or her criteria for success.

8-35

Would you describe for me the action of a person who previously performed poorly in this position?

This question gives the hiring manager an opportunity to reflect on his or her criteria for failure.

5 BEST QUESTIONS ABOUT THE HIRING MANAGER'S MANAGEMENT STYLE

8-36

How would you describe your own management style?

This is the most direct statement of the question.

8-37

What are the most important traits you look for in a subordinate?

The hiring manager has a lot of latitude with this question. Listen for terms such as "loyalty."

8-38

How do you like your subordinates to communicate with you?

You'll get a sense of how formal or informal your prospective manager prefers to be.

8-39

What personal qualities or characteristics do you most value?

This question will solicit important information about the personal qualities that the hiring manager will reward.

8-40

Could you describe to me your typical management style and the type of employee who works well with you?

You're going to be working closely with this hiring manager. It's important to know his or her management style. If there's going to be a conflict between your styles, it's better that you know that now.

Memorably Good Question
#10

What's the most important thing I can do to help within the first 90 days of my employment?

This question is particularly smart because by answering it, the interviewer has to assume the candidate is already on board.

Kimberly Bedore
Director, Strategic HR Solutions
Peopleclick
Dallas, TX

10 BEST QUESTIONS ABOUT CORPORATE CULTURE

8-41

Corporate culture is very important, but it's usually hard to define until one violates it. What is one thing an employee might do here that would be perceived as a violation of the company's culture?

This question reveals a sophisticated understanding of corporate culture as a force most easily observed in its violation. Typical responses are lying and other ethical breaches, but listen for other clues.

8-42

How would you characterize the organization? What are its principal values? What are its greatest challenges?

This profound question demonstrates your deep interest in the organization's makeup.

8-43

How would you describe the experience of working here?

Here's a question that goes to the interviewer's experience of corporate culture.

8-44

If I were to be employed here, what one piece of wisdom would you want me to incorporate into my work life?

This is a strong question that not only asks the hiring manager what he or she considers most important but also assumes that you are already on board.

8-45

What are a couple of misconceptions people have about the company?

Every manager is frustrated by the way he or she thinks the world sees the company. Here is your chance get two pieces of critical information: how the hiring manager thinks the world perceives the company and what he or she believes to be the truth.

8-46

Work-life balance is an issue of retention as well as productivity. Can you talk about your own view of how to navigate the tensions between getting the work done and encouraging healthy lives outside the office?

On one level, you want to find out how workaholic your prospective manager and the company are. On another, you want a clue about how the company handles the important issue of work-life balance.

8-47

How does the company support and promote personal and professional growth?

This is another way to ask how the company culture promotes a healthy work-life balance.

8-48

What types of people seem to excel here?

This will engender more conversation about personality styles and attitudes that mesh well with the culture and those that don't. You bluff your way through this question at your own risk. Why would you want to go to work where you would be at war with the prevailing culture?

8-49

Every company contends with office politics. It's a fact of life because politics is about people working together. Can you give me some examples of how politics plays out in this company?

It's a slightly risky question because "politics" has such a negative connotation. But the reality is that every organization is a political organization. The politics at family-owned companies is much different than the politics of large multinational companies. The issue is, with which are you more comfortable?

8-50
What have I yet to learn about this company and opportunity that I still need to know?
A great open-ended question for the interviewer to elaborate on an important point you might not have considered.

25 BEST QUESTIONS ABOUT GENERAL BUSINESS OBJECTIVES

8-51
I'm delighted to know that teamwork is highly regarded. But evaluating the performance of teams can be difficult. How does the company evaluate team performance? For example, does it employ 360-degree feedback programs?
While many companies talk about the importance of teamwork, they reward individual performance. It's unlikely that teamwork can really be transformational unless teams are evaluated and rewarded.

Memorably Bad Question
#12

What's your policy on dating coworkers?

What's with this guy? What is his motivation for working here? There were many questions that went through my head, none of which I could ask. The question left a bad taste in my mouth for the rest of the interview. He was not offered a job.

Bryan Debenport
Corporate Recruiter
Alcon Laboratories
Fort Worth, TX

8-52

What are the organization's primary financial objectives and perform-ance measures?

The question combines an understanding that objectives are meaning-less without measures.

8-53

What operating guidelines or metrics are used to monitor the planning process and the results?

This follow-up question probes for specifics on how the organization determines success.

8-54

To what extent are those objectives uniform across all product lines?

Here is a follow-up question that probes for discontinuities in the or-ganization, not an uncommon situation in a corporation formed as the product of multiple mergers and acquisitions.

8-55

How does the company balance short-term performance versus long-term success?

This is a tough question for every executive.

8-56

What kinds of formal strategic planning systems, if any, are in place?

The Internet revolution relegated formal strategic planning systems such as management by objective to the sidelines, but with the dot-com melt-down, they are starting to come back.

8-57

Can you describe the nature of the planning process and how decisions concerning the budgeting process are made?

This question is a little more granular, with an emphasis on the budget.

8-58

Can you identify the key corporate participants in the planning process?

This is a variation of the planning question, this time in human terms.

8-59

How often and in what form does the company report its results internally to its employees?

Look for an answer that involves the word "intranet."

8-60

In the recent past, how has the company acknowledged and rewarded outstanding performance?

This question can put the interviewer in a tough spot. If the company has enjoyed good results, you are asking for specific ways the company has shared the wealth with employees. If results have not been good, you are asking for an acknowledgment that there was nothing to share.

8-61

What are the repercussions of having a significant variance to the operating plan?

You are asking how the company deals with failure.

8-62

Are budgeting decisions typically made at corporate headquarters, or are the decisions made in a more decentralized fashion?

The answer to this question reveals how "top down" decision making is at the company.

8-63

I'm glad to hear that I will be part of a team. Let me ask about reward structures for teams. Does the company have a formal team-based compensation process?

A big issue for companies is that they pay lip service to the team effort but reward people as individuals. Here's an exception to the rule about not asking compensation questions before the interviewer brings up the subject.

8-64

Is the company more of an early adapter of technology, a first mover, or is it content to first let other companies work the bugs out and then implement a more mature version of the technology?

This question tells the hiring manager not only that you are thinking about technology, but that you get a clue about whether the company is a leader or prefers to follow.

8-65

How does the company contribute to thought leadership in its market?

This is an elegant way of inquiring about the company's commitment to a leadership position in articulating the issues of the industry. How important is it for you to be part of such an intellectual environment? Can you contribute?

8-66

A company's most critical asset is its knowledge base. How advanced is the company's commitment to knowledge management?

This question demonstrates a high level of thinking about an emerging competency: the management of actionable knowledge so that it can be used across the company.

8-67

I was pleased to hear you describe the company's branding strategy. How does branding fit into the overall marketing mix?

Branding is, like "quality" or "customer service," a value that everyone in the company should be building. Be sure you have something to say about branding before you bring up a question like this.

8-68

How does this position contribute to the company's goals, productivity, or profits?

This is a variation on a very strong question that links the position and the company's hot buttons in a way that lets you speak to your strengths.

8-69

According to (name source), your principal competitor, Brand X, is the best-selling product in the space. What does Brand X do better than your product?

A provocative question, it is true, but it's no news to the interviewer. The question shows that you have done your research and suggests that you understand the company can't improve unless it understands what the competition does better. The hope is that you have some salient experience you can offer in this regard.

8-70

Business Week *magazine ranks the company second (or whatever) in its industry. Does this position represent a change from where it was a few years ago?*

You probably should know the answer to this question, but the point is to start a conversation about the momentum of the company. Is its rank going up or down, and how does the interviewer deal with it?

8-71

How accessible is the CEO (name him or her) to people at my level of the organization?

At some firms, CEOs meet with new employees as well as established employees. Some CEOs have an open-door policy and some are remote figures. How does it work here?

8-72

Does the CEO (name him or her) publish his or her email address?

If you want to work for a nonhierarchical company with an open-door policy, look for a CEO who welcomes email. A CEO who does not welcome email, or, worse, does not have email, indicates a more structured organization.

 ## Memorably Bad Question

#13

Have you been playing pocket pool?

The candidate shook hands with the hiring manager, conspicuously wiped his hands on his trousers, and delivered the above question with a smirk. He was escorted out shortly thereafter.

HR manager for a *Fortune* 500 telecommunications company
Requested anonymity

8-73

I understand that the CEO is really approachable. Are there ground rules for approaching him or her?

Even the most accessible CEO needs staff to be thoughtful.

8-74

Staff development is mentioned in your annual report as a measure on which executives are evaluated. What kinds of training experiences might I expect?

The question indicates deep interest in the company, an understanding of the link between staff development and success, and a focus on staff development in the service of the company's long-term objectives as much as on the individual's development.

8-75

Is the department a profit center?

Departments or work units organized as profit centers generate their own revenue, making them much less at risk for layoffs.

5 BEST QUESTIONS ABOUT COWORKERS

8-76

Can you please tell me about the people who will look to me for supervision.

A teamwork question. It's very important to know whom you will be supervising. As well, this question also exposes the people who may not report directly to you but will nevertheless see you as a leader.

8-77

Would I encounter any coworker or staff person who's proved to be a problem in the past?

Oh boy, now you're getting into dicey territory. Still, it's worth asking. Shows you understand that every organization struggles with interpersonal issues. If the hiring manager looks around and gives you an honest answer to this question, you are looking very good. If you have your notebook out, put it away.

8-78

What happened to the person who previously held this job?

This question launches a very important conversation. You'll learn either that this is a new position, that the incumbent resigned or was dismissed, or that the incumbent was promoted. You can then offer any of these follow-ups.

8-79

The incumbent was dismissed? What did you learn from the incident? How could the problems have been avoided?

You want to be seen as interested in the incident as a learning opportunity, not as a rubbernecker at a highway car crash. The issue is what the hiring manager learned and what you can take away from the incident.

8-80

The incumbent was promoted? I'm delighted to hear it. Would it be possible for me to talk to him or her?

This is excellent news. Not only might the incumbent be made available to you, but the position seems to be a launching pad for career success. Getting the opportunity to talk to the person who held the job you want is gold. Redouble your request.

6 BEST QUESTIONS ABOUT CUSTOMER SERVICE

8-81

What is the company's customer service philosophy?

Customer service is the mantra of most companies, and this high-level question can open a conversation about customer service. If you ask this question, make sure you have something valuable to say about what you can deliver in this area.

8-82

Could you tell me about a time when the team/company went out of its way to provide knock-your-socks-off service?

People love showing off if they are coaxed. Listen carefully to the story, and be prepared to offer a similar story where you were the hero.

8-83

The best companies rely on rich customer data to fuel personalized content and services. How is the company doing in personalizing its offerings?

The question demonstrates your understanding of how the Internet has changed marketing and customer service. Be prepared to demonstrate how you can advance the company in its personalization objectives.

8-84

Customers are expecting companies to protect their data. Does the company have a privacy policy for its Web initiatives, and how does the company balance the momentum for ever-increasing personalization with rising concerns for privacy?

If you ask this question, be sure you have some concrete experience in this area.

8-85

How empowered are employees? How much of the company's money can your people (including the ones with single-digit pay grades) spend on their own recognizance to satisfy a customer or address a work-process issue?

You are asking for evidence that the organization pays more than lip service to employee empowerment.

8-86

How often would I come into direct contact with real, living, breathing, paying customers?

This question goes to how much the organization trusts its employees. Exposing customers to employees can be risky, but without significant customer contact, no employee can appreciate what it really means to be successful.

6 BEST QUESTIONS FOR COMPANY FOUNDERS AND OWNERS

If your interview is with the founder or owner of the company, especially if your position proposes to take on activities currently handled by the founder or owner, you have a special challenge.

All the other questions in this book are fair game, and will give you good information. But the main challenge of working with a company founder or owner is not in getting the job offer, but in succeeding at the job. If it doesn't work out, often it won't be because of performance but because of the inability of the company founder or owner to let go of the reins. Thus, the questions you ask in this circumstance need to give you sharp information about fit.

Business history shows that few company founders have the skills to manage the company when it gets past a certain size. Few such managers, however, acknowledge this reality. One of your main goals in the interview, then, is to try to determine how you will be able to work with this individual and, by extension, his or her heirs, all of whom have a stake in the business. To satisfy yourself of the viability of the situation, you are entitled to a much greater degree of latitude.

Company founders and owners have tremendous pride in the success of the organizations they built. They will generally resist sharing their organizations with anyone else. The big issue, then, is how willingly the company founder or owner is prepared to adjust the company's balance of power and, perhaps, ownership. The questions that follow are designed to give you a clue about how flexible the company founder or owner might be. The questions assume the candidate is interviewing for a senior executive position, perhaps the COO to the founder's CEO. Use these wordings as the basis for customizing questions to your unique situation:

8-87

What are the success factors that will tell you that the decision to bring me on board was the right one?
This question starts the conversation off on the success factors that you will bring to the organization.

8-88

How would you describe the company you'd like to leave your heirs in terms of sales, size, number of employees, and position in the industry?
This opens the conversation about heirs and what impact they may have on the negotiations.

8-89

Have you considered the degree to which you want your heirs to have strategic or operational influence in the company until one of them is ready to assume the role of COO or CEO?

If there is an heir waiting in the wings, this is a good way to start a conversation about it.

8-90

If for any reason you were unable to function as CEO, how would you like to see the company managed? Is this known, understood, and agreed to by your heirs? Is it in writing?

Transition strategies, or more frequently the lack of them, derail many organizations. If a transition strategy exists in writing, you can have some confidence that the organization is relatively mature in its governance.

8-91

To make our working relationship successful—something we both want—we'll need to be sure we have good chemistry together. How might we determine this, and then what action would you see us engage in to build that relationship?

This question alerts the CEO that one of your success factors is the relationship between the two of you.

8-92

If you and I were developing some sort of philosophical difference, how would you want to go about resolving it?

Here is a refreshingly candid question that goes to how inevitable differences will be resolved.

QUESTIONS FOR PRIVATE COMPANIES

Public companies—those raising funds by selling stock—are by law required to disclose certain aspects of their ownership, organization, and financial results. Private companies are not required to do so, and many such firms stay private precisely because they prefer to protect such details. You, however, need to understand certain details of how the company is funded and organized so you can make an informed decision about whether it's a good fit for you. If you want to make the best decision possible for yourself, there is no alternative but to ask. The more senior the position you are applying for, the more expected it is for you to ask the hard questions. Many of the questions in this book are appropriate for public and private companies, but the following questions are targeted for private companies only:

- Is the company profitable?
- How is the company funded?
- Who are the investors?
- How are corporate decisions made?
- How is the company organized?
- What is the company's burn rate?
- How much money does the company have in the bank?
- What are the growth opportunities?
- Has the company considered filing for an IPO (initial public offering)?
- Is private stock available to me? What about stock options?
- Has the company been approached for a merger or takeover?
- What was the company's reaction to the merger or acquisition overture?
- Has that attitude changed?
- Where do you see the company (or function) going in the next three years?
- Can you tell me about the company's roots?

As former president Ronald Reagan would say, "Trust, but verify." Asking these questions is just the first step. Confirming the accuracy of the answers is the second.

PART III

THE QUESTION LIFE CYCLE

You have two critical purposes in asking questions. At first, you want every question to sell yourself. At some point, you also want to ask questions to help you decide if you really want the position. After all, as the interview progresses, you are becoming an investor in the company, investing with the most valuable assets you have: your time, talent, and allegiance.

FOUR GROUPS OF QUESTIONS

There are four groups of questions you can pick from when it's your turn to ask questions, and each is the subject of one of the next four chapters. *Exploring* questions do double duty: They demonstrate your interest in the job and the company, and they help you learn more about the opportunity. *Defensive* questions let you know what you're getting into and protect you from making a mistake. *Feedback* questions are really sales techniques to identify objections and solidify your position. *Bid-for-action* questions are designed to clinch the offer. I am indebted to Gary Ames, vice president of consulting at Merrill-Adams in Princeton, New Jersey, and Dr. Wendell Williams, managing director of ScientificSelection.com in Atlanta, Georgia, for the organization of these questions.

Part III concludes with questions you can ask after you have received an offer—and in the event you didn't receive an offer—what you can do to leverage rejections.

IF THE CULTURE FITS

Most organizations hire on ability and fire on fit. By the same token, most employees choose companies on the basis of salary and benefits and quit on the basis of culture and interpersonal relationships. Thus one of your main goals in questioning, besides making yourself look interested and attractive, is to determine if the company offers a culture that you can work with. There is no route more certain to lead to despair and turnover than bluffing your way into a company whose culture is at war with your own.

One way to gauge a company's culture is by asking a series of questions and then filling out a company culture survey. This culture survey was developed by Empyrean Consulting, Inc., a staffing firm in Dallas, Texas, to help its candidates determine the culture of the company they are considering. Empyrean understands that without a good cultural fit, the prospects for long-term satisfaction are reduced. At this point, take a few minutes to complete the survey.

COMPANY CULTURE SURVEY

Instructions: Assuming you are comfortable with the culture of your current or last position, complete the survey based on your current or last position. Then go back and complete the survey on the basis of your understanding of what the culture in the new position is. Alternatively, if you are not currently employed or are unhappy with your position, complete the survey on the basis of your "wish list" for your next company. Then go back and complete the grid based on your estimation of the company culture you are considering joining.

Work Styles

Describe the work style of the company or team.

Decisions made independently				Decisions made as a team
1	2	3	4	5

Tasks limited to job description				Perform duties outside normal job scope
1	2	3	4	5

IT-Business Relationship

Describe the relationship between the IT department and other parts of the business.

Assignments from IT				Assignments from business unit
1	2	3	4	5

Responsible to IT				Responsible to business unit
1	2	3	4	5

Formal development/change management processes				Informal development/ change processes
1	2	3	4	5

Little contact with business units				Significant contact with business units
1	2	3	4	5

Worker Relationships

Describe the relationship among the coworkers.

Typical coworker education level: High school				Typical coworker education level: Graduate school
1	2	3	4	5

Employees eat lunch together				Employees eat lunch at desk
1	2	3	4	5

Employees engage in after-work activities (e.g., softball league)				Little or no after-work activities
1	2	3	4	5

Collegial				Independent
1	2	3	4	5

Company Relationship

Which of the following attitudes best describes the culture?

Employees are expected to adhere to a fixed work schedule				Employees can set their own schedule as long as the work is done
1	2	3	4	5

Employees must schedule and clear all time off				Employees may take unplanned time off/vacation days
1	2	3	4	5

The company has implemented formal policies and procedures				Policies and procedures are mostly informal, unwritten
1	2	3	4	5

Atmosphere

Describe the general working atmosphere of the company.

Formal				Casual
1	2	3	4	5

Big business				Entrepreneurial
1	2	3	4	5

Highly structured				Chaotic
1	2	3	4	5

High pressure				Laid back
1	2	3	4	5

Scoring. If there is reasonable agreement between the two sets of marks, you can have confidence that the cultures of the two companies are similar. If you succeeded in one, it is likely you will be successful in the other. But watch out if there is a radical disconnect between the two sets of marks. That means the behaviors that have stood you in good stead in your last company may well create friction for you in the new one. Changing cultures is not necessarily a bad thing, but doing so without awareness is a prescription for disappointment.

CHAPTER 9

EXPLORING QUESTIONS

SHOW YOUR INVESTMENT IN THE JOB AND LEVEL THE PLAYING FIELD

Exploring questions probe for details about the job, company, management, and people you would be working with. Even more, these questions demonstrate that you have invested in researching the company. This levels the power between you and the interviewer, who now is uncertain about how much you already know about the company. As a general rule, approach these questions about products, customers, and processes as would a consultant. You are the expert engaged in an informational interview so that you can render an expert opinion.

Of course, no one would ever ask all these questions in one job interview, but you want to get a good understanding of four aspects: the job, the people, the management, and the company. Before your next interview, select four or five of these questions and reword them to meet the unique requirements of the individual interview.

8 BEST QUESTIONS ABOUT THE POSITION

9-1
May I see a job description? What are the most important responsibilities of the job?
A good place to start is to ask for a job description.

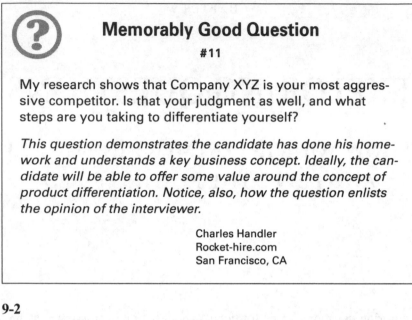

Memorably Good Question

#11

My research shows that Company XYZ is your most aggressive competitor. Is that your judgment as well, and what steps are you taking to differentiate yourself?

This question demonstrates the candidate has done his homework and understands a key business concept. Ideally, the candidate will be able to offer some value around the concept of product differentiation. Notice, also, how the question enlists the opinion of the interviewer.

Charles Handler
Rocket-hire.com
San Francisco, CA

9-2

How much time should be devoted to each area of responsibility?
This question asks the interviewer to identify what is most important and then to prioritize. Often interviewers will find this question very difficult because they don't really know. But how can you succeed without agreements on what's most important?

9-3

What initial projects would I be tackling?
Like the question above, this is another attempt to prioritize, this time looking at projects.

9-4

What is my spending/budget authority?
This question goes to how much responsibility you will have before bumping into someone else's responsibility.

9-5

What are you hoping to accomplish, and what will be my role in those plans?
You want to know what the company's strategic goals are and how the company hopes you will contribute.

9-6

Presuming that I'm successful on this assignment, where else might I be of service to the company?
First things first, of course, but the question will tell the interviewer that you have a long-term perspective.

9-7

Can you please describe the management team to me?
This is the most general question about the management team you will report to.

9-8

Can you show or sketch me an organizational chart?
An organizational chart is a road map to the company's structure and how much authority you will have.

10 BEST QUESTIONS ABOUT INFORMATION TECHNOLOGY

9-9

Will I receive my assignments from IT or from the business unit?
This is a critical question that goes to the very DNA of the information technology resource in the company. Organizations in which the business units have significant input into the technology agenda are generally much more responsive to market conditions than organizations in which IT is more insulated from business realities. On the other hand, the IT function can be a lot more volatile. Which environment do you prefer?

9-10

Do developers have little contact with the business unit or significant contact?
This variation of the above question looks at IT contact with business units as a measure of how responsive IT is.

9-11

Does the company have a Net-use policy? May I see it?
The answer to this question will give you a good clue about what levels of trust operate in the company. An overly retroactive Net policy may point to a company that is uncomfortable with the uncertainties of the Net.

Memorably Good Question

#12

Do you have any questions or concerns about my ability to perform this job?

A candidate is always better off bringing objections out in the open. A stated objection may be addressed. Unstated objections will sink you every time.

Scott Hagen
Senior Internet Recruiter
Recruiters-Aid
San Marcos, CA

9-12

To whom does the chief information or technology officer report?

If the CIO reports directly to the CEO, this indicates a company that places high strategic value in the IT function.

9-13

What are the biggest technical challenges ahead for this department/ company?

Get a sense of how the hiring manager defines the technical challenges and be prepared to sell yourself against those outcomes.

9-14

Traditionally, companies have used IT to reduce bottom-line costs. But I am excited about the use of IT to advance top-line opportunities such as creating new products and identifying new markets. Can you talk about how IT is used in this company to create top-line value?

Do you want to work in a company where IT continues to be an inward-facing function?

9-15

What structured strategies for software testing have you found effective here?

Note that this is a question that makes sense only with an interviewer who has a passion for software testing.

Memorably Good Question

#13

When top performers leave the company, why do they leave and where do they usually go?

This is tough for the interviewer to answer because she might not want to identify the company that seems to get the top performers. But if she is as confident about her company as she is about you, she will assume you already know about that company and that it is probably also considering you. The implicit question is, Why should I work for your company instead of the other one?

John Sullivan
Professor, Human Resources Management
San Francisco State University
San Francisco, CA

9-16

Does the company use an IT steering committee?

The question demonstrates understanding of how some companies develop IT funding and strategies.

9-17

Do you have a formal development change management process, or is the process more informal?

Many developers hate formal, structured processes or standards; others welcome the structure. Be clear about the environment you are considering joining.

9-18

After months of working long hours, the morale of IT workers can plummet. What rewards have you found effective in recognizing and rewarding exceptional work?

This question can be made more perceptive if you actually have some concrete suggestions for monetary as well as nonmonetary methods for recognizing performance. Who knows, you may end up on the receiving end of what you suggest.

Memorably Bad Question
#14

May I work on Christmas Day?

Bizarre. We appreciate the dedication, but we also want our employees to have lives.

ACT-1 Recruiter, Phoenix, AZ

5 BEST QUESTIONS FOR SALES AND MARKETING POSITIONS

9-19
What is the commission structure, and what is my earning potential in 1, 3, 5, or 10 years?
Every salesperson needs to understand how commissions and related compensation work.

9-20
If you put all the salespeople in a line from your best to the merely acceptable performer, what are the earnings of the 50th percentile? The 25th? The 75th?
This is a good way to understand your earning potential if you join the company.

9-21
What percentage of salespeople attain objectives?
Every salesperson has a quota. If a larger percentage of salespeople fail to meet quota, it indicates that either the quota is too high or the sales team is inadequate.

9-22
What percentage of the current people are above and below their set goals?
In other words, how does the company handle underperforming salespeople?

9-23
Can you describe the performance of the sales team?
You want to know whether you will be joining a team of superstars or
also-rans.

ADDITIONAL EXPLORING QUESTIONS

- To whom would I report?
- How many direct reports will I have?
- What is the background of those I would supervise?
- Would it be possible to meet the people who work in the department?
- What is the average turnover in the department I hope to join?
- How many new hires per year does it take to keep the department fully staffed?
- How would you describe the corporate culture (or work environment) here?
- What do you like best/least about working for [manager's name]?
- How responsive is management to employee ideas?
- How much interaction do you have with supervisors and other coworkers?
- Do you work more on an independent basis or in a team environment?
- How would you describe the corporate culture (or work environment) here?
- How does your organization differ from its competitors?
- What are the company's plans for future growth?
- What problems is your organization facing?
- What do you like most about working here?
- What is the size of the division, its sales volume, and its current earnings?
- What is the 5- to 10-year company plan?

- How are you positioned in relation to your competitors?
- What kind of support does the company provide for research and development?
- What do you like about living in this community?
- Does the company have structured pay levels?
- What percentage of my time would be spent in the various functions you described that this job involves?
- How much contact is there between departments (if a large organization)?
- How would you describe the culture of your organization?
- What's the best way to become familiar with corporate policies, practices, and culture?
- Where does this position fit into the structure of the department and the organization as a whole?

CHAPTER 10

DEFENSIVE QUESTIONS

QUESTIONS THAT LET YOU KNOW WHAT YOU'RE GETTING INTO AND PROTECT YOU FROM MAKING A MISTAKE

Defensive questions are designed to make sure you want the job. By this time, the organization has either offered you the job or expressed a strong interest in your qualifications. Relish it. You will never be in a position of greater strength. Now is the time to ask the tough questions that will give you the information on which you can make the best decision for your career.

Even if you are unemployed, resist the temptation to take the job just because it is offered. You may be in the frying pan now, but the fire is surely hotter if you accept a job you don't fully understand. So ask away.

While you never want to ask questions that spoil your rapport with the interviewer, make it clear that you expect candid answers to your queries. Actually, there is an advantage to being real at this point. Most interviewers expect you to look out for your interests. If you can't speak up for your own interests, they will figure, how can you be expected to speak out for the best interests of the organization?

Here is where your research protects your interests. You need to know why the company is losing money, why the prior incumbent quit, and what are the relocation plans for the department. It is perfectly appropriate to ask to speak with potential subordinates and colleagues. They are excellent sources of information; they know what is going on

Memorably Good Question

#14

What was the last fun thing that you did that wasn't work-related?

I had made it through a series of interviews for a position in New York City that paid about $60,000 per year. After interviewing with the manager and owner of the company, I had a gut feeling that they expected employees to work 14-hour days plus weekends. How could I ask a question about work hours without appearing lazy or like a clock-watcher? So at the end of my third interview, I asked the manager that question. Her face turned a bit sullen as she said, "Well, I had fun at the company business party we had on our business trip to Canada." From that one question, I learned that if I accepted the position, I'd be signing my life away to this company.

Bob Johnson
Director of Public Relations
St. Bartholomew's Church
New York, NY

and are most likely going to be straight with you. You may ask these people about the informal power structure, the unwritten priorities, what it really takes to be successful, and what they most want to change.

15 BEST DEFENSIVE QUESTIONS

10-1

If I were a spectacular success in this position after six months, what would I have accomplished?

This is a very bold way to understand the "dream list" of accomplishments you will, on some level, be expected to fulfill.

10-2

Do you foresee this job involving significant amounts of overtime or work on weekends?

It's a fair question, so ask it straight.

10-3

I understand the company has experienced layoffs within the last two years. Can you review the reasons why they were necessary?

It will make the interviewer uncomfortable, but the interviewer expects questions about layoffs

10-4

How were the layoffs handled in terms of notification, severance, out-placement services, etc.?

You want to know how your termination, should you be downsized, will likely be handled.

10-5

Are there formal metrics in place for measuring and rewarding performance over time?

The impression you want to leave is that you are good and you want the metrics to recognize it.

10-6

How effectively has the company communicated its top three business goals?

If the interviewer cannot articulate them, you have your answer.

10-7

I am a hard worker. I expect to be around other hard-working people. Am I going to be comfortable with the level of effort I find here?

 Memorably Bad Question

#15

Before you tell me about your benefits, can I go get my wife? She's in the car and she's the one who wants to know about the benefits.

Maybe she should be the one applying for the job.

Wayne Kale
Ryon Recruiters
Hendersonville, NC

You are asking the interviewer if you will find the kind of hard-working environment in which you thrive at this position. If the interviewer hedges at all, you have your answer.

10-8
Is the company's training strategy linked to the company's core business objectives?
The most sophisticated companies do link their training and education investments to core business objectives.

10-9
How does your firm handle recognition for a job well done?
The way an organization rewards achievement tells you a lot about its culture.

10-10
When was the last time you rewarded a subordinate for his or her efforts? What token of appreciation did you offer?
This question goes from the general to the specific. You are now asking about the manager's practices in rewarding subordinates.

10-11
How does the firm recognize and learn from a brave attempt that didn't turn out quite as expected?
Many companies say they have a nonpunitive attitude toward managers who make mistakes, but few live up to the attitude. Ask about a time when the lessons from a mistake were widely disseminated across the organization.

10-12
How much freedom would I have in determining my objectives and deadlines?
This question goes to how much authority you will have to do your job in the manner you see fit versus working to someone else's preferences.

10-13
How long has this position existed in the organization? Has its scope changed recently?
Information about the history of the position and its recent evolution can influence your decision.

Memorably Bad Question
#16

I have custody of my niece and can get child care only three days a week. Can I bring her to work with me the other days?

We want to be sensitive to child-care issues, but we also expect candidates to have these issues under control.

> Richard Kathnelson
> VP of Human Resources
> Syndesis, Inc.
> Ontario, Canada

10-14
What are the greatest challenges I will face in this position in furthering the agenda of the organization?
The question asks the interviewer to identify the obstacles, impediments, and other land mines that people occupying every position in an organization must confront. If the interviewer suggests there are no such obstacles, you know it's a lie.

10-15
Are my tasks limited to my job description, or will I be performing duties outside the described job scope?
If there is a job description, it is frequently ignored. If you're going to be doing your job as well as someone else's, you should know now, before you accept the job.

CHAPTER 11

FEEDBACK QUESTIONS

QUESTIONS THAT INDICATE AND SOLIDIFY YOUR POSITION

Ed Koch, a former New York mayor, made famous this quip: "How'm I doing?" You should pepper your conversation with forms of this question as well. Feedback questions allow you to uncover and disarm an interviewer's concerns.

It is often extremely difficult to learn what the interviewer doesn't like about you. In many cases, company policy or fear of litigation prevents interviewers from giving you information that is critical for you to know if you are to improve your interviewing techniques. "Candidates need to understand that providing honest feedback is really tricky for recruiters and sometimes impossible," says Janice Brookshier of Seattlejobs.org. "If you received a bad reference, for example, I can't tell you."

However, you must uncover doubts, if they exist. I believe that the facts are friendly. They may not always be convenient. If you have been fired or been in jail or have a big gap in your work history, these facts are not pleasant. But they are friendly because you have control over their disclosure. You are always better off dealing with the facts than hoping they will be ignored. Facts may not be discussed, but they are never ignored.

The point is that you can't address an objection you don't know about. These questions require courage. Don't be afraid of letting your weaknesses surface. You want to be in the position of overcoming objections since this is when selling occurs.

10 BEST FEEDBACK QUESTIONS

11-1

How do you like me so far?

A cheeky question at its best, but if said with a smile and a light tone of voice, it might work.

11-2

Do you have any concerns about my ability to do the job and fit in?

This is an important question because it shows humility and gives you the opportunity to both address and eliminate an objection.

11-3

Is there anything standing in the way of us coming to an agreement?

Notice the question isn't about the offer, it's about agreement.

11-4

Do you have any concerns about my experience, education, skills?

This is a direct question about any objections the interviewer might have.

11-5

How do I compare with the other candidates you have interviewed?

Here's another way to look at where you stand, and it's always good to get information on the competition.

11-6

Describe your ideal candidate. What do my qualifications lack compared with those of the theoretical ideal candidate?

Ⓧ Memorably Bad Question

#17

I don't have any experience, so can I get a job in management?

That might be hard. You may be overqualified.

ACT-1 Recruiter
Mountain View, CA

Memorably Bad Question

#18

What do you pay me if you fire me?

Don't worry. We'll never have to deal with that issue.

ACT-1 Recruiter
Phoenix, AZ

If you get a sense that the interviewer thinks you are underqualified, here's a question that might give you a shot at persuading him or her that you have what it takes.

11-7
Is there anything else I can elaborate on so that you would have a better understanding of my qualifications and suitability for this position?
The answer often reveals where the interviewer is less than totally comfortable with your credentials.

11-8
Are there any areas in which you feel I fall short of your requirements?
You're making a direct appeal to the interviewer to talk about your shortcomings. Now show the interviewer how you can listen to criticism without getting defensive.

11-9
Can you give me any feedback that would make me more attractive to the company in the future or that I could benefit from next time?
If you don't get the job, maybe this question will at least give you some vital feedback you can use for next time.

11-10
Is there anything else you need from me to have a complete picture of my qualifications?
This is an alternative and elegant formulation of the central feedback question.

CHAPTER 12

BID-FOR-ACTION QUESTIONS

QUESTIONS THAT CLINCH THE OFFER

Jobs interviews are sales calls. The product you are selling is yourself. Marketing 101 says that every marketing message needs a bid for action: a clearly worded request for the order. Pick up the phone. Send in the response card. Click on the link. Give me an offer.

So it is with each job interview. Each time you meet with a hiring manager, you have an irreplaceable opportunity to ask for the offer.

"When I'm interviewing a candidate for a sales position, I want them to close me," says Bob Conlin, VP of Incentive Systems in Bedford, Massachusetts. "If they give me a soft close, or, worse, no close at all, I get concerned." Here's an example of what Conlin considers to be a hard close:

Bob, every year I'm going to be your number-one guy. Every year I'm going to beat quota. I'm your candidate. When can I start?

"I know I'm being closed here," he says. "The candidate is speaking my language. His confidence is infectious."

But Conlin also wants to see evidence that the candidate is mindful of the organization's goals, not just the salesperson's goals. The following question is even more thoughtful because it demonstrates that the candidate is already thinking as a member of a team:

I know I can drive the revenues and net the customers. What kinds of processes are in place to help me work collaboratively?

Besides asking for the job, bid-for-action questions ask for an indication of how favorably the interviewer assesses you. One way to assess a company's interest is to see how hard the interviewer tries to sell you on accepting the job when you ask these questions. Some candidates grow pale at saying something as blatant as:

Are you ready to make me an offer now, or do I need to sell myself some more?

But what do you have to lose? If the job you are applying for has any marketing or management quality at all, the interviewer will be impressed by your confidence. Every great salesperson knows to "ask for the order." Here's how to ask for the job in the final interview. Begin with a statement of your understanding of the opportunity:

As I understand it, the successful candidate will be someone with x education, y qualifications, and z experience. Do I understand the opportunity correctly?

Here your purpose is threefold. First, you are testing to see if you indeed understand the situation. If you missed something, or, more likely, the interviewer forgot some important requirement, now is the time to get it right. Second, assuming you summarized the position correctly, the interviewer is impressed by your organizational skills. Third, asking for agreement at this point is a strategy for getting the interviewer into the habit of saying yes. Yes is the answer you want to the next question, and it's good to have the interviewer in a yes mood.

The critical next question is:

Do I meet the requirements?

Now wait. That's the hard part. The interviewer is making up his or her mind. The answer will tell you if it is time to close or if you have more persuading to do. If the interviewer is positive and says that, yes (there's that word again), you have all the qualifications, you can now deliver the strongest closing line there is:

I'm glad we agree. I feel that way, too. So I am certainly interested in receiving your strongest offer.

But I must issue a fair warning. You are on dangerous ground here. Your decision to ask for the job must be pitch-perfect. Before asking for the job, you must have created a good rapport with your interviewer, established that you are a good fit for the job, and extracted at least some expression of interest from the interviewer. Your timing must be so perfect the interviewer could set her watch by it. In other words, unless you have a high degree of confidence about each of these points, I wouldn't take a chance.

It's a risky move for two reasons:

First, while asking a prospect to say yes to an order for a gross of pens with the business's logo emblazoned on them might occasionally get the prospect to sign on the bottom line, it's highly unlikely that you will actually get a hiring manager to say, "Sure, you want the job? You got it! When can you start?" Even the hiring manager has a process to go through and must consult with others. Still, asking for the job might move you up in the crowd.

And second, it might blow you out of the water. That's because in contemporary American business culture, asking for something as important as a job is loaded with a lot of emotional baggage. It's

Memorably Good Question
#15

What do you see in me? What are my strongest assets and possible weaknesses? Do you have any concerns that I need to clear up in order to be the top candidate?

A totally confident question that asks the hiring manager to encapsulate your qualifications. It concludes with a strong bid for action.

John Sullivan
Professor, Human Resources Management
San Francisco State University
San Francisco, CA

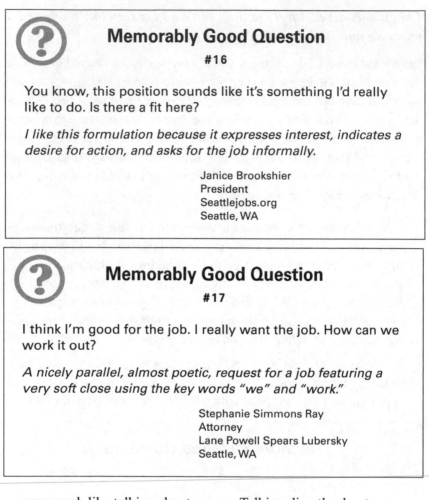

Memorably Good Question

#16

You know, this position sounds like it's something I'd really like to do. Is there a fit here?

I like this formulation because it expresses interest, indicates a desire for action, and asks for the job informally.

Janice Brookshier
President
Seattlejobs.org
Seattle, WA

Memorably Good Question

#17

I think I'm good for the job. I really want the job. How can we work it out?

A nicely parallel, almost poetic, request for a job featuring a very soft close using the key words "we" and "work."

Stephanie Simmons Ray
Attorney
Lane Powell Spears Lubersky
Seattle, WA

very much like talking about money. Talking directly about money is taboo. Everyone knows it's the most important part of the conversation in a job interview, yet the pretense we all have about money relegates it to the end, almost as if money were an afterthought.

So it is with the business of directly asking for a job. Still, the benefits usually outweigh the risks. If your tone is pitch-perfect and your timing is right, asking for the job will help differentiate your credentials from the crowd, reinforce your value proposition, and in extremely rare cases, even land you an offer on the spot.

WHAT RECRUITERS THINK

Asking for the job directly is tricky, and there's some disagreement from recruiters and job coaches. Some consider asking for the job assertive; others think it cheeky or smacking of desperation. My personal preference is to err on the side of being assertive. The meek may, as the Bible says, inherit the earth, but they don't necessarily get jobs. As always, you have to use your radar and trust your instincts.

It's good to be direct when asking for the job, says Tony Stanic, resource manager at CNC Global, in Ottawa, Ontario, Canada. "I think it is good to come across as enthusiastic and direct as possible. The person that appears to want the job the most will get the offer. Try to find out their level of interest in you by asking them directly." Stanic has been impressed with candidates who could deliver lines such as:

- Do you feel that I am suitable for the position?
- Do you have any reservations about my ability to do this job?

"Don't be afraid to ask these questions," Stanic continues. "You may be able to overcome any objections that they may have. It may feel a bit uncomfortable but it's better to find out what their concerns are than it is to find out that you did not get the job. Asking for the job can be a crucial factor in the interviewer's decision-making process."

"There's a fine line between confidence and arrogance," says KnowledgePoint's HR director, Rich Franklin. To be successful in some jobs, you need to be pushy and demonstrate in the job interview how aggressively you can sell. For example, Franklin recruited stockbrokers for Dean Witter for 10 years before he joined KnowledgePoint. Stockbrokers, of course, are salespeople who sell securities. One question from a sales candidate that that impressed him was:

- I'm the person for the job! Can you tell me when you can make me an offer?

"In the software industry where things are more laid back," Franklin continues, "I'd be a little less comfortable with a guy coming on that strong."

The Pacific Firm's Nancy Levine also urges caution. For her, such direct questions are indications of too much thinking inside the box. What Levin likes to hear from candidates are more subtle probes for objections:

- I am very interested in this position. Do you have any questions or concerns I can address?
- It has been a pleasure meeting you. I really want this job. Can you tell me where you are in your process?

"Then, hopefully, the interviewer will cough up objections that the job-seeker can address and overcome," Levine says.

The important thing, she says, is not to appear like you're trying too hard. For example, Levine criticizes a formulation such as this:

As I understand it, the successful candidate will be someone with x education, y qualifications, and z experience. Do I understand the opportunity correctly?

"For me this formulation is too cookie cutterish, too car salesman-y, a bit transparent in terms of trying to close," she says. "It may work as a line of questioning in a first phone call, but not to close in an interview. I would expect that our discussion would pinpoint what we're looking for."

 Memorably Bad Question

#19

I just want to get rich and then get out. How long will that take?

Why wait? Get out now.

Bob Conlin,
VP, Incentive Systems
Bedford, MA

Memorably Bad Question
#20

If I work here, would I get an office or a cubicle? I'd really like to be able to close the door.

Who wants to hire someone who closes the door before he is hired? The candidate has closed the door on any chances of getting an offer.

Susan Trainer
Senior Information Systems Recruiter
RJS Associates
Hartford, CT

"There has to be a certain chemistry between me and the candidate for those kinds of questions to come off well," agrees Kimberly Bedore, director of Strategic HR Solutions at Peopleclick, Dallas, Texas. "You have to know the interviewer is really interested; otherwise it makes the interviewer uncomfortable." Don't put the interviewer in a defensive mode, she adds. "Just demonstrate that you understand the company's greatest business problem and that you have what it takes to solve it. Asking for what the next step will be is always okay."

So the burden is on you to call it right. If your timing is even slightly off or your voice is a little too shrill, you will come off as grasping, clumsy, or, worst of all, desperate. If you're going to ask for a job, please practice these questions with a trusted friend or mentor. Use a video camera to record yourself uttering the questions. Until you can pull off a vibe of relaxed confidence, I'd avoid these questions.

BUT SALES JOBS ARE DIFFERENT

In general, as we discussed, it's tricky to be too direct in asking for the job. But if you are applying for any kind of sales representative job, then asking for the job is not optional. If you don't ask for the job in the interview, you probably won't get it. The employer wants you to be able to close the sale. Why should the employer give you a chance selling his or her product or service when you can't even sell yourself? Remember, the job of a sales representative is to ask for the order and to close the deal, not just make a nice presentation. For sales interviews, phrases like these may be appropriate:

- I really want this job. Am I going to get it?
- I think I earned this job. When am I going to receive an offer?
- Did I get the job?
- I'd like to start right away. When can we get the paperwork out of the way?

The following bid-for-action questions give you some wordings to ask for the job with varying degrees of directness. Each one of the questions can serve as a proactive close to the main part of the interview. Each of these questions has been field-tested and, in the right circumstances, has been shown to work. In other cases, the questions may backfire. The risk is that the interviewer may regard you as cheeky or insolent. Study the situation well and tread lightly.

10 BEST BID-FOR-ACTION QUESTIONS

12-1
Is there anything personally or professionally that you believe would prevent my being a solid contributor in this role?
If not, you can assume that the next step is working out the hiring details. If yes, then you are positioned to address the objection.

12-2
Mr. Employer, your search is over. You will not find anyone else more qualified to do this job than I. If I were you, I'd cancel all the other interviews and make me an offer.
This approach can be considered either confident or cheeky. But in the right tone of voice, it can be effective.

Memorably Bad Question

#21

How long it is going to be, exactly, before I get a job from your company?

We couldn't say, exactly, but don't hold your breath.

ACT-I Recruiter
Denver, CO

12-3

Mr. Employer, I'm not going to keep it a secret. I really want this job, and I know I will be fantastic in it.

Now shut up and listen. Resist the temptation to justify this bold statement. If you are in a dead heat with two other candidates, all other things being equal, you can bet that the most enthusiastic job seeker will get the nod.

12-4

Until I hear from you again, what particular aspects of the job and this interview should I be considering?

Notice how confident the question is. It's not "if" but "when." The question deftly reminds the interviewer that just as the company is considering you, you are considering the company.

12-5

I know I can meet the demands of the position and would make an outstanding contribution. Can I have the offer?

Confronted so directly, the interviewer must make a statement about your chances of being hired. If the interviewer doesn't, he or she isn't interested in you at all.

12-6

What will be your recommendation to the hiring committee?

Phrased like this, you are flattering the interviewer that his or her recommendation is valuable.

12-7

I'm ready to make a decision based on the information I have. Is there anything else you need to make me an offer?

An effective one-two punch of a question that combines an expression of interest with a subtle invitation to see an offer.

12-8

I am very interested in this job, and I know your endorsement is key to my receiving an offer. May I have your endorsement?

Phrased this way, the question does not request that the interviewer offer a job, but merely the endorsement. It also flatters the interviewer by making it clear that his or her recommendation carries considerable weight, whether it does or not.

12-9

It sounds to me as if we have a great fit here. What do you think?

Note that this is very aggressive phrasing, perhaps best suited for a sales position.

12-10

It has been an interesting and fruitful discussion. I would very much like to take it to the next step.

This is a statement rather than a question, but it closes the interview very effectively by not only requesting a next step, but assuming that there will be one.

CREATING A SENSE OF URGENCY

If you want to push the interviewer for a decision, you can apply some subtle pressure by using one of the questions below. You will create a sense of urgency that might prompt the interviewer to come back with an offer quicker than he or she might have. But it also introduces a lot of risk. The interviewer may feel pressured or even bullied. Do it only when you can afford to lose—if you in fact have other offers in the bank or you are comfortably employed. These four closes put a little heat on the interviewer:

- I have other offers pending that afford me tremendous potential. But I like what I see here, and I know I'm the right person for you. If you agree, can we talk turkey?

- Is there anything I have said that indicates I am not the perfect candidate for this job?

- I am in final-stage interviews with other companies, but I like what I see here. I'd like to have an offer from you so I can make a decision.

- Based on my family's needs and other interviews, I am committed to making a decision by next Friday. What do we have to do to speed up the decision-making process so that I might consider an offer from you by that time?

CHAPTER 13

QUESTIONS FOR SUPERSTARS

BONE-CHILLING QUESTIONS FOR WHEN THEY KNOW YOU'RE THE BEST

Superstars, the most highly sought after candidates, can afford to be picky. Even in today's economy, the competition for the most talented contributors is brisk. For that reason, superstars can ask prospective employers questions that other candidates would have a hard time getting away with. "Superstars can interview the company with bone-chilling questions to make sure they select the best opportunity offered them," says Dr. John Sullivan, professor and head of Human Resource Management at San Francisco State University. The following are the types of questions that the most confident candidates routinely ask, according to Dr. Sullivan.

"Even if you aren't a superstar (yet), it's important to be skeptical because recruiters and hiring managers, on occasion, make jobs appear better than they really are," Sullivan says. "You need an accurate job preview, and it takes hard questions to your future manager to get it. The hiring manager's ability and willingness to answer these tough questions should be a major factor in your decision to accept an offer."

There's no reason why you cannot act like a superstar and put some of these questions in your portfolio. Who knows? Maybe if you act like a superstar, they will treat you as one.

THE COMPANY

13-1

What's the gross profit margin of the division I will be working in? What percentage of the total profit from the company does it generate? Is it increasing or decreasing?

It's critical to know the contribution of your division or department to the total profit of the organization.

13-2

What's your company's "killer application"? What percentage of the market share does it have? Will I be working on it?

Every company has a core product that often generates the lion's share of the revenues. If that's where you want to be, make sure that's where you will be placed.

13-3

Can you give me some examples of the best and worst aspects of the company's culture?

Does the hiring manager have enough insight to know that every corporate culture has both positive and negative qualities?

13-4

What makes this company a great place to work? What outside evidence (rankings or awards) do you have to prove this is a great place to work? What is the company going to do in the next year to make it better?

This is a fairly aggressive question, but if it's fair for the company to ask you to prove you are the best, the reverse is also true.

13-5

What would I see if I stood outside the front door at five o'clock? Would everyone be smiling? Staying late or leaving early? Would everyone be taking work home?

Why not conduct this experiment before you ask the question? See if the interviewer's answer squares with your observations.

13-6

Lots of your competitors have great products and people programs. What is the deciding factor that makes this opportunity superior? Are you will-

ing to make me some specific "promises" on what you will do to make this a great experience for me if I accept the position?

The superstar is asking for the interviewer to "sell" the company.

13-7

Can you show me that the company has a diverse workforce and that it is tolerant of individual differences? Does it have affinity groups or similar programs that I might find beneficial? Is there a dress code? Can you give me an example of any "outrageous conduct" this firm tolerates that the competitors would not?

How tolerant is the company for the kind of chaos that many superstars generate in the course of greatness?

13-8

Does your company offer any wow! benefits? Does it pay for advanced degrees? Does it offer paid sabbaticals? On-site child care? Relocation packages? Mentor programs? How are these superior to those of your competitors? What about job sharing? Flex-time arrangements? Telecommuting? Workout facilities?

If these practices are important to you, by all means ask.

13-9

When top performers leave the company, why do they leave and where do they usually go?

This is tough for the interviewer to answer because he or she doesn't want to give you names of other employers to consider. But if the interviewer is confident in her case, she will.

13-10

When was the last significant layoff? What criteria were used to select those to stay? What packages were offered to those who were let go?

Layoffs are a fact of life even in the most stable companies. It's fair game to talk about the company's management of layoffs.

13-11

Does the company have a program to significantly reward individuals who develop patents/great products? Is there a program to help individuals "start" their own firms or subsidiary? Will I be required to fill out noncompete agreements?

You plan to generate great intellectual property for the company. It's fair to know how those assets will be managed.

THE JOB AND
THE DEPARTMENT

13-12
How many approvals would it take (and how long) to get a new $110,000 project idea of mine approved? What percentage of employee-initiated projects in this job were approved last year?
Ask for examples. If you want to be part of a nimble organization, this is a great way to ask.

13-13
How many days will it take for you (and the company) to make a hiring decision for this position?
The superstar might as well have said "hours." Organizations these days know they have to move quickly to snag the best candidates.

13-14
Who are the "coolest" people on my team? What makes them cool? Can I meet them? Who is the best and worst performer on the team, and what was the difference in their total compensation last year? Sell me on this team and the individuals on it that I get to work with. What makes my closest coworkers fun or great people to work with?
A complicated question, but all focused on understanding the makeup of the team you will be joining. These are the people who will determine whether you succeed or fail.

13-15
What is your "learning plan" for me for my first six months? What competencies do you propose I will develop that I don't currently have? Which individual in the department can I learn the most from? What can he or she teach me? Can I meet that person? Does the company have a specific program to advance my career?
These questions pin the company down on resources for advancing your portfolio of skills.

13-16

Assuming I'm current with my work, how many days could I not show up at the office each week? Could I miss a day without your advance permission? What percentage of the people in this position telecommute? Has anyone in the group been allowed to take a month off (unpaid) to fulfill a personal interest?

If personal autonomy is important to you, get it on the table and determine if there is precedent for what you want. It's much easier to follow precedent than to create it.

13-17

Give me some examples of the decisions I could make in this job without any approvals. Can you show me the degree of autonomy and control I will have in this position?

This is another way to ask how the company values personal autonomy.

13-18

How many hours a week do you expect the average person on your team to work? How many hours does the average person in fact work? Are there work-life programs in place to promote a healthy work-life balance?

As a superstar, you are prepared to put in the hours—you just want to know what they are.

13-19

How will my performance be evaluated? What are the top criteria you use? What percentage of my compensation is based on my performance? Is there a process where the employees get to assess their supervisor? If I do a great/bad job in the first 90 days, how, specifically, will you let me know? What are the steps you would take to help me improve? How do you discipline team members?

The answers to this complicated set of questions should tell you how the company evaluates and motivates performance as well as how it corrects lack of performance.

13-20

What is the first assignment you intend to give me? Where does that assignment rank on the departmental priorities? What makes this assignment a great opportunity?

You want to know if you will be immediately contributing to an important, visible project.

13-21
How many hours of your time can I expect to get each week for the first six months on the job? How often will we have scheduled meetings?
You want to know how much face time you will have with your manager.

13-22
If I were frustrated about my job, what specific steps would you take to help me overcome that frustration? How about if you were frustrated with me? Can you show me examples of what you have done for others in your group in the past year to overcome any frustration?
This is a supremely confident question that is frank in assuming there will be occasional frustrations. The bigger issue is what services are in place to help resolve frustrations.

13-23
What are the wows! of this job? What are the worst parts? And what will you do to maximize the former and minimize the latter? If I asked the incumbent what stinks about the job, what would he or she say? Can I talk to him or her?
This balanced but nevertheless threatening question asks for the good, the bad, and the ugly. Every company is made up of all three qualities. The bigger issue is whether the hiring manager has the spine to be up front about it.

13-24
What will make my physical work environment a fun and stimulating place to spend time?
If the physical workspace is important to you, ask. This general question is better than asking about air hockey tables or company masseurs.

13-25
What inputs do employees get in departmental decisions? In hiring and assessing coworkers?
You'll want to know about all-important team processes. Make sure you ask for specifics.

13-26

Could I get a chance to see the team in action? Can I sit in on a team meeting? Shadow someone for a day?

Is the interviewer willing to make the company more transparent to you? This is a good way to find out.

13-27

What are the biggest problems facing this department in the next six months and in one year? What key competencies have you identified that I will need to develop in the next six months to be successful?

Here you're looking for the hiring manager's hot buttons. These are the issues against which your initial performance will be evaluated.

13-28

What do you see in me? What are my strongest assets and possible weaknesses? Do you have any concerns that I need to clear up in order to be the top candidate? What is the likelihood, in percent terms, that you will make me an offer?

This is a bold and confident bid for action question that also asks for any objections.

13-29

What is the best/toughest question I could ask you to find out about the worst aspects of this job? How would you answer it? If you were my best friend, what would you tell me about this job that we haven't already discussed?

A last-ditch attempt to reveal negative information about the company.

CHAPTER 14

YOU GOT AN OFFER. CONGRATULATIONS!

NOW'S THE TIME TO ASK ALL THOSE QUESTIONS YOU WANTED TO ASK

Now that you have an offer or a strong expression of interest, it's appropriate to ask questions about compensation, benefits, and the community in which you will be working. Before you ask questions, take a close look at the written letter of confirmation and compensation summary that the employer will give you. These materials will address most of your questions. If not, by all means ask to speak with someone in human resources to satisfy yourself. By the time you make a decision, you should have details on all of these issues.

COMPENSATION

- What are my salary, commissions, and other compensation?
- How often will I be paid?
- Am I entitled to stock options?
- Am I entitled to noncash compensation?
- Am I entitled to the use of a company vehicle?

BENEFITS

- What are the insurance benefits to which I am entitled?
  - Life insurance?
  - Major medical?
  - Surgical?
  - Hospitalization?
  - Disability?
  - Dental?
  - Mental health?
  - Eye care?
- What is the extent of these coverages?
- What will be my cost for carrying these coverages?
- Are my dependents covered?
- Is there extra cost for dependent coverage?
- Is there a retirement plan?
  - If so, is it contributory or noncontributory?
  - What is the employee's contribution amount?
  - What is the retirement benefit amount?
  - Is it funded with pretax dollars?
- Is there a 401(k) plan?
  - If so, what are the details?
- Is there a stock purchase plan?
- Does the company match contributions?
- Is there a charitable gift–matching program?
- Is there paid sick leave?
  - If so, how does it work?
- Is there a tuition reimbursement plan?
- Are there company paid holidays? What are they?

- What is the company's vacation policy?
- What other benefits does the organization provide?

RESTRICTIONS

- Do I have to sign an employment contract?
- Do I have to sign a noncompete agreement?
- Do I have to sign a net-use policy?
- Do I have to assign rights to intellectual property?

MOVING EXPENSES

Conversations about moving expenses, like benefits, are premature until after the company has made you an offer or expressed strong interest. Relocating an employee is expensive, and few companies will enter into it lightly. The company's willingness to do so puts you in a position of power. Now is the time for you to gain a complete understanding of how the company treats relocation expenses. There is a wide variety of practice in this area, so be clear. Many company relocation policies address such points as:

- Do you provide reimbursement of closing costs for the sale of my old house?
- Do you provide reimbursement of closing costs for the purchase of my new house?
- Will the company assist in the sale of my current house?
- If I can't sell my old house, do you have a program that will buy it?
- Can the company provide a loan for buying a house? If so, what are the terms?
- If I need to rent while looking for a house, will I be reimbursed?
- Does the company pay for house-hunting trips in the new community? How many?

- Does the company provide reimbursement for temporary living expenses? Any limitations?
- Does the company provide reimbursement for the shipment of household goods?
- Does the company provide reimbursement for the storage of household goods?
- Does the company provide reimbursement for the shipment of family vehicles?
- Does the company provide reimbursement for the tax gross-up of the taxable portion of moving expenses?
- In the event my landlord is unwilling to release me from my lease, will the company assume the obligation for the lease?

THE COMMUNITY

Only after significant mutual interest is established or an actual job offer is in hand should you ask questions about the community where you will be living and working. The precious time of the interview is better spent on establishing mutual interest. There will be ample time to collect this information after the interview. Of course, the company will have a lot of material promoting the community in which it operates. But also collect independent information from real estate agents, chambers of commerce, and other responsible agencies. The following is a checklist of issues you should be conversant with as you and your family make a decision. Most of these issues deal with cost.

HOUSING OR RENTAL COSTS

- Mortgage costs
- Real estate taxes
- Home owner insurance
- Utility costs
- Electricity

Memorably Good Question

#18

Who are the "coolest" people on my team? What makes them cool? Can I meet them?

A confident "superstar" question that demonstrates that you understand that the team you work with will make all the difference in your success.

John Sullivan
Professor, Human Resources Management
San Francisco State University
San Francisco, CA

- Water
- Heat
- Natural gas
- State income taxes (if any)
- Local income taxes (city, county, township)
- Personal property taxes (if any)
- Other assessments of taxes
- Commuting costs

OTHER ISSUES

- Public schools
- Commute
- Crime rate
- Culture
- Worship
- Hospitals

CHAPTER 15

YOU BLEW THE INTERVIEW. NOW WHAT?

LEVERAGE REJECTION INTO A LEARNING EXPERIENCE

No one likes to be rejected, but if you are serious about your career in the long term, you must learn to embrace rejection. In the course of your career you will get rejected for a lot of reasons—some valid, some not so valid—and sometimes for no reason at all. The challenge of embracing rejection is to accept your limitations, transform hopelessness into action, and learn from each rejection. Allow me to rephrase the celebrated serenity prayer:

Grant me the confidence to accept the rejection I cannot change, the determination to change the rejection I can, and the wisdom to learn from each.

When they are rejected, most candidates fold up their tents and slink away. That is understandable, but precisely the wrong strategy. To a salesperson, a no is just the beginning of another conversation. Many candidates have parlayed a rejection into a relationship that led to another job offer, if not for the original job then for another job. Even if you can't do this, a rejection can be beneficial if you can get authentic feedback.

Your first challenge is to find out why you were rejected. Be honest with yourself as you think about it. Oftentimes you will know why. You were underqualified, you were overqualified, or your previous salary was too high or too low. These objections were surely brought out in the interview, so your rejection should have been no major surprise. You can take some comfort from the fact that there was nothing much you could have done to overcome these objections.

Every once in a while, you will blow an interview, quickly realize what you did wrong, and kick yourself immediately afterward. You might recover from some of these mistakes, but others are fatal, at least as far as that job is concerned. Perhaps you dressed inappropriately. Or perhaps you inadvertently insulted the interviewer. Perhaps you permitted yourself a moment of anger to vent at your current supervisor. Maybe you were late to the interview or were unprepared because you didn't have any questions to ask. By the time you left the interview, you knew it was hopeless. Consider these learning experiences and resolve to conduct yourself more professionally next time.

But occasionally a rejection will come out of left field, and you will feel blindsided because you just didn't see this one coming. You felt you were well qualified for the job. The interviewer seemed to like you and gave you some positive indications that everything was going to work out. You left the interview feeling positive. Then you get a letter or phone call telling you thanks, but no thanks.

UNDERSTANDING REJECTION

This is the time when embracing rejection pays off. You have to understand exactly why you were rejected. There is really only one way to do this. You have to ask the person who rejected you why.

Susan Trainer suggests that if a candidate is rejected, he or she send should a short note that conveys the following thoughts:

Thank you again for interviewing me. I understand you decided to go with another candidate and I accept your decision. I'd appreciate any feedback you can give me.

Key here is acknowledging that you accept the interviewer's decision. The issue of your application for this position has been decided. You lost. Get over it. No recruiter will help you if he or she thinks you want to argue.

Unfortunately, many interviewers are not going to tell you what you want to know under any circumstances. The fear of lawsuits by former employees has so traumatized employers that they will almost never give candidates the authentic feedback they need. Some companies are so fearful that an HR person may inadvertently say something that might come back and bite them that they sharply restrict what HR people can say. Companies checking references on former employees run into this problem all the time. Many companies now reveal only the title of former employees and the dates of their hire and termination. Reluctantly, they may reveal salary information. In fact, a new trend at some companies is to have reference checks conducted entirely by a computerized telephone system that gives prospective employers the minimal information. The idea is to remove the actual HR people from the process.

In this atmosphere it is all but impossible to get a hiring manager or HR person to be honest. It's a shame, because many HR people are educators by nature and desperately want to tell candidates what they could do better next time or how their résumé could be improved. But they have absolutely no incentive to do so and lots of incentive to keep mum. For you, that makes getting authentic feedback very difficult.

An HR manager at a *Fortune* 1000 company who prefers not be identified reported the following exchange with a candidate who had just received a letter of rejection:

CANDIDATE: Thanks for taking my call. I got your letter telling me that you won't be making me an offer. I was a little surprised because I left the interview thinking that I was very qualified for the job. Of course, I accept your decision, but I am calling to try to understand why I did not get an offer. I want to learn from any mistakes I may have made. Candidly, can you tell me why I did not get the offer and what I might have done differently to present myself as a stronger candidate?

WHAT THE INTERVIEWER WANTED TO SAY: I admire you for making a call like this. It takes a thick skin to ask for such details. In fact, you sabotaged yourself in a number of ways that can be easily remedied. You had a couple of misspelled words on your résumé and your choice to wear sandals instead of shoes caused some of us to question your professionalism.

WHAT THE INTERVIEWER ACTUALLY SAID: I appreciate your call, and we were impressed by your credentials, but the truth is that another candidate simply had a little more experience in the areas most important to us. Good luck in your job search.

Unless you have a personal relationship with the hiring manager, it's almost impossible to get honest feedback about the selection process. And the irony is, the more you need brutally honest feedback—the more there's something you can actually do something about—the less chance you will get it. That's because few HR professionals want to come clean on the subjective reasons one candidate is chosen over another.

HR people can afford to be a little more honest about objective standards. Let's say you lost the job because it called for five years of C++ experience and you only had two years. That they might tell you. If the job calls for a commercial driver's license and you don't have one, that they'll tell you. If the job requires a Microsoft certification and you don't have one, that they'll tell you. But you probably knew all that already. If you were rejected on any type of subjective basis, forget it.

Here's where a recruiter intermediary can be helpful. No one likes to give bad news directly to a candidate. But if an interviewer knows the recruiter is willing to communicate the bad news, then the interviewer may be more willing to tell the truth. Susan Trainer remembers that a well-qualified candidate for a position as a hospital administrator was rejected for a particular job for which he was well qualified. When she inquired, the hospital interviewer disclosed that the candidate asked to smoke during the interview. It was clear that the interviewer would not have revealed that critical fact directly to the candidate. Trainer then had the unenviable task of confronting the candidate with the costs of his addiction. But the candidate learned, took control of his addiction, and soon got a well-paying position.

Sometimes the subjectivity of hiring managers can be unreasonable. Jason Rodd, senior consultant at TMP Worldwide, Inc., in Tampa,

Florida, recalls working with a hiring manager who rejected a perfectly qualified candidate because, well, let Rodd tell it:

> I couldn't understand why she was rejected because she could do the job with her eyes closed. After pressing for a reason, the hiring manager eventually told me it was because the candidate wore a turtle broach on her suit. Turns out he did not like turtles and questioned her professionalism for wearing a turtle to a job interview. There is no way the candidate would have gotten that feedback directly. I tell candidates that story from time to time because I want them to know that it is the little things that can get you ruled out late in the game.

CUTTING THROUGH THE PRETENSE

There is one strategy for cutting through the pretense, but it's pretty strong medicine and it doesn't always work. Of course, you have little to lose. I personally have had success with it, so I know it can pay off. After you are rejected for a position and you genuinely don't know why, call the interviewer. The pitch goes something like this:

Thanks for taking my call. I got your letter telling me that you won't be making me an offer and I accept the decision. I need to improve my interviewing skills and I'm asking for your help. I am asking you to be brutally honest about my performance and what I could have done better. I can make you three promises. I promise I will not interrupt you. I promise I will not defend myself. And I promise I will not contact you or your company for a year. Will you help me?

That last appeal is important. It speaks to the desire of most HR people to be helpful.

"I would be totally impressed with a candidate who came at me like that," says Rich Franklin, HR director at KnowledgePoint in Petaluma, California. Like many HR people, Franklin is an educator. "This is a guy that wants to learn. If an HR person is any good at all, they would jump at that opportunity," he adds.

The key to success with this approach is to give the recruiter enough comfort so that his desire to be honest with you overcomes his reluctance to get into trouble. Most interviewers faced with a rejected candidate fear three things: an argument, a sob story, or a pest who might sue. Acknowledging that you accept the recruiter's decision and will not try to appeal it is the first step. The three promises you make up front are further designed to counter these fears. The promise that you will not contact the interviewer is key. That gives a little assurance that what the interviewer tells you won't come back and bite him or her. Don't forget, the company is still free to contact you.

If you're going to try this strategy, I ask only one thing: Demonstrate integrity. If you promise not to interrupt, bite your tongue and don't interrupt. If you promise not to defend yourself, stick to your promise. It won't be easy. Few of us have the constitution to listen to criticism without trying to explain or justify. Just listen and say thank you. Take what you learn and do better next time.

ENLARGE THE RECRUITER'S TERRITORY

Whether you get a job offer or not, follow up with a thank-you letter. You'd be surprised how few candidates actually take this simple step. Most recruiters tell rejected applicants they will keep their résumés on file, and a few actually mean it. But if you send a great letter accepting the recruiter's decision and suggesting that if another position more suitable opened up you would very much like for the company to consider you, chances are much greater that the recruiter would follow through.

In addition to a thank-you letter, consider leaving the recruiter better off for having interviewed you. You can enlarge the recruiter's territory—and perhaps put yourself in his or her debt—by taking one or more of these steps:

- If you know of one, recommend another good candidate for the job.
- If you can offer some other relationship like a sales lead, do it.
- If you know of a new Web site or job board, alert the recruiter.
- Send an article or Web link you think the recruiter might find helpful.

- If nothing else, ask if there is anything you can do to help the recruiter or his or her company.

Remember, vision is good, but it doesn't get you anywhere unless you combine it with action and a questioning attitude. Listen more than you speak and every venture will bear fruit. Good luck with job search.

10 FINAL TIPS FOR ASKING POWERFUL QUESTIONS

1. Do your homework.
2. Write down at least four questions in advance of the interview.
3. Listen twice as much as you talk.
4. Don't ask a question unless you are certain the answer will make you appear engaged, intelligent, qualified, and interested in taking the job.
5. Never initiate "what about me?" questions.
6. Take notes using a professional-looking notebook and pen.
7. Don't interrupt.
8. Don't argue.
9. Ask for the job.
10. Silence your cell phone or pager.

INDEX OF QUESTIONS

201 BEST QUESTIONS
TO ASK ON YOUR
INTERVIEW

7-9

I have really enjoyed meeting with you and your team, and I am very interested in the opportunity. I feel my skills and experience would be a good match for this position. What is the next step in your interview process?

7-10

Before I leave, is there anything else you need to know concerning my ability to do this job?

7-11

In your opinion, what is the most important contribution that this company expects from its employees?

7-12

Is there a structured career path at the company?

7-13

What are my prospects for advancement? If I do a good job, what is a logical next step?

7-14

Assuming I was hired and performed well for a period of time, what additional opportunities might this job lead to?

7-15

Do the most successful people in the company tend to come from one area of the company, such as sales or engineering, or do they rise from a cross section of functional areas?

7-16

I know that for the position for which I am interviewing, the company has decided to recruit from outside the organization. How do you decide between recruiting from within and going outside?

7-17

How does this position relate to the bottom line?

7-18

What advice would you give to someone in my position?

7-19

How did you get into your profession?

7-20

What major problems are we facing right now in this department or position?

7-21

Can you give me a formal, written description of the position? I'm interested in reviewing in detail the major activities involved and what results are expected.

7-22

Does this job usually lead to other positions in the company? Which ones?

7-23

Can you please tell me a little bit about the people with whom I'll be working most closely?

7-24

As I understand the position, the title is ____, the duties are _____, and the department is called _____. I would report directly to _____. Is that right?

7-25

Can you talk about the company's commitment to equal opportunity and diversity?

7-26

Who are the company's stars, and how was their status determined?

7-27

How are executives addressed by their subordinates?

7-28

What can you tell me about the prevailing management style?

7-29

If you hired me, what would be my first assignment?

7-30
Does the company have a mission statement? May I see it?

CHAPTER 8

8-1
What specific skills from the person you hire would make your life easier?

8-2
What are some of the problems that keep you up at night?

8-3
What would be a surprising but positive thing the new person could do in the first 90 days?

8-4
How does upper management perceive this part of the organization?

8-5
What do you see as the most important opportunities for improvement in the area I hope to join?

8-6
What are the organization's three most important goals?

8-7
How do you see this position impacting on the achievement of those goals?

8-8
What attracted you to working for this organization?

8-9
What have you liked most about working here?

8-10
In what ways has the experience surprised or disappointed you?

8-11
What are the day-to-day responsibilities I'll be assigned?

8-12

Could you explain the company's organizational structure?

8-13

What is the organization's plan for the next five years, and how does this department or division fit in?

8-14

Will we be expanding or bringing on new products or new services that I should be aware of?

8-15

What are some of the skills and abilities you see as necessary for someone to succeed in this job?

8-16

What challenges might I encounter if I take on this position?

8-17

What are your major concerns that need to be immediately addressed in this job?

8-18

What are the attributes of the job that you'd like to see improved?

8-19

What is your company's policy on attending seminars, workshops, and other training opportunities?

8-20

What is the budget this department operates with?

8-21

What committees and task forces will I be expected to participate in?

8-22

How will my leadership responsibilities and performance be measured? By whom?

8-23

Are there any weaknesses in the department that you are particularly looking to improve?

8-24

What are the department's goals, and how do they align with the company's mission?

8-25

What are the company's strengths and weaknesses compared with the competition (name one or two companies)?

8-26

How does the reporting structure work here? What are the preferred means of communication?

8-27

What goals or objectives need to be achieved in the next six months?

8-28

Can you give me an ideal of the typical day and workload and the special demands the job has?

8-29

This is a new position. What are the forces that suggested the need for this position?

8-30

What areas of the job would you like to see improvement in with regard to the person who was most recently performing these duties?

8-31

From all I can see, I'd really like to work here, and I believe I can add considerable value to the company. What's the next step in the selection process?

8-32

How does this position contribute to the company's goals, productivity, or profits?

8-33

What is currently the most pressing business issue or problem for the company or department?

8-34
Would you describe for me the actions of a person who previously achieved success in this position?

8-35
Would you describe for me the action of a person who previously performed poorly in this position?

8-36
How would you describe your own management style?

8-37
What are the most important traits you look for in a subordinate?

8-38
How do you like your subordinates to communicate with you?

8-39
What personal qualities or characteristics do you most value?

8-40
Could you describe to me your typical management style and the type of employee who works well with you?

8-41
Corporate culture is very important, but it's usually hard to define until one violates it. What is one thing an employee might do here that would be perceived as a violation of the company's culture?

8-42
How would you characterize the organization? What are its principal values? What are its greatest challenges?

8-43
How would you describe the experience of working here?

8-44
If I were to be employed here, what one piece of wisdom would you want me to incorporate into my work life?

8-45
What are a couple of misconceptions people have about the company?

8-46

Work-life balance is an issue of retention as well as productivity. Can you talk about your own view of how to navigate the tensions between getting the work done and encouraging healthy lives outside the office?

8-47

How does the company support and promote personal and professional growth?

8-48

What types of people seem to excel here?

8-49

Every company contends with office politics. It's a fact of life because politics is about people working together. Can you give me some examples of how politics plays out in this company?

8-50

What have I yet to learn about this company and opportunity that I still need to know?

8-51

I'm delighted to know that teamwork is highly regarded. But evaluating the performance of teams can be difficult. How does the company evaluate team performance? For example, does it employ 360-degree feedback programs?

8-52

What are the organization's primary financial objectives and performance measures?

8-53

What operating guidelines or metrics are used to monitor the planning process and the results?

8-54

To what extent are those objectives uniform across all product lines?

8-55

How does the company balance short-term performance versus long-term success?

8-56

What kinds of formal strategic planning systems, if any, are in place?

8-57

Can you describe the nature of the planning process and how decisions concerning the budgeting process are made?

8-58

Can you identify the key corporate participants in the planning process?

8-59

How often and in what form does the company report its results internally to its employees?

8-60

In the recent past, how has the company acknowledged and rewarded outstanding performance?

8-61

What are the repercussions of having a significant variance to the operating plan?

8-62

Are budgeting decisions typically made at corporate headquarters, or are the decisions made in a more decentralized fashion?

8-63

I'm glad to hear that I will be part of a team. Let me ask about reward structures for teams. Does the company have a formal team-based compensation process?

8-64

Is the company more of an early adapter of technology, a first mover, or is it content to first let other companies work the bugs out and then implement a more mature version of the technology?

8-65

How does the company contribute to thought leadership in its market?

8-66

A company's most critical asset is its knowledge base. How advanced is the company's commitment to knowledge management?

8-67
I was pleased to hear you describe the company's branding strategy. How does branding fit into the overall marketing mix?

8-68
How does this position contribute to the company's goals, productivity, or profits?

8-69
According to (name source), your principal competitor, Brand X, is the best-selling product in the space. What does Brand X do better than your product?

8-70
Business Week *magazine ranks the company second (or whatever) in its industry. Does this position represent a change from where it was a few years ago?*

8-71
How accessible is the CEO (name him or her) to people at my level of the organization?

8-72
Does the CEO (name him or her) publish his or her email address?

8-73
I understand that the CEO is really approachable. Are there ground rules for approaching him or her?

8-74
Staff development is mentioned in your annual report as a measure on which executives are evaluated. What kinds of training experiences might I expect?

8-75
Is the department a profit center?

8-76
Can you please tell me about the people who will look to me for supervision?

8-77

Would I encounter any coworker or staff person who's proved to be a problem in the past?

8-78

What happened to the person who previously held this job?

8-79

The incumbent was dismissed? What did you learn from the incident? How could the problems have been avoided?

8-80

The incumbent was promoted? I'm delighted to hear it. Would it be possible for me to talk to him or her?

8-81

What is the company's customer service philosophy?

8-82

Could you tell me about a time when the team/company went out of its way to provide knock-your-socks-off service?

8-83

The best companies rely on rich customer data to fuel personalized content and services. How is the company doing in personalizing its offerings?

8-84

Customers are expecting companies to protect their data. Does the company have a privacy policy for its Web initiatives, and how does the company balance the momentum for ever-increasing personalization with rising concerns for privacy?

8-85

How empowered are employees? How much of the company's money can your people (including the ones with single-digit pay grades) spend on their own recognizance to satisfy a customer or address a work-process issue?

8-86

How often would I come into direct contact with real, living, breathing, paying customers?

8-87

What are the success factors that will tell you that the decision to bring me on board was the right one?

8-88

How would you describe the company you'd like to leave your heirs in terms of sales, size, number of employees, and position in the industry?

8-89

Have you considered the degree to which you want your heirs to have strategic or operational influence in the company until one of them is ready to assume the role of COO or CEO?

8-90

If for any reason you were unable to function as CEO, how would you like to see the company managed? Is this known, understood, and agreed to by your heirs? Is it in writing?

8-91

To make our working relationship successful—something we both want—we'll need to be sure we have good chemistry together. How might we determine this, and then what action would you see us engage in to build that relationship?

8-92

If you and I were developing some sort of philosophical difference, how would you want to go about resolving it?

CHAPTER 9

9-1

May I see a job description? What are the most important responsibilities of the job?

9-2

How much time should be devoted to each area of responsibility?

9-3

What initial projects would I be tackling?

9-4

What is my spending/budget authority?

9-5

What are you hoping to accomplish, and what will be my role in those plans?

9-6

Presuming that I'm successful on this assignment, where else might I be of service to the company?

9-7

Could you please describe the management team to me?

9-8

Can you show or sketch me an organizational chart?

9-9

Will I receive my assignments from IT or from the business unit?

9-10

Do developers have little contact with the business unit or significant contact?

9-11

Does the company have a Net-use policy? May I see it?

9-12

To whom does the chief information or technology officer report?

9-13

What are the biggest technical challenges ahead for this department/ company?

9-14

Traditionally, companies have used IT to reduce bottom-line costs. But I am excited about the use of IT to advance top-line opportunities such as creating new products and identifying new markets. Can you talk about how IT is used in this company to create top-line value?

9-15

What structured strategies for software testing have you found effective here?

9-16
Does the company use an IT steering committee?

9-17
Do you have a formal development change management process, or is the process more informal?

9-18
After months of working long hours, the morale of IT workers can plummet. What rewards have you found effective in recognizing and rewarding exceptional work?

9-19
What is the commission structure, and what is my earning potential in 1, 3, 5, or 10 years?

9-20
If you put all the salespeople in a line from your best to the merely acceptable performer, what are the earnings of the 50th percentile? The 25th? The 75th?

9-21
What percentage of salespeople attain objectives?

9-22
What percentage of the current people are above and below their set goals?

9-23
Can you describe the performance of the sales team?

CHAPTER 10

10-1
If I were a spectacular success in this position after six months, what would I have accomplished?

10-2
Do you foresee this job involving significant amounts of overtime or work on weekends?

10-3

I understand the company has experienced layoffs within the last two years. Can you review the reasons why they were necessary?

10-4

How were the layoffs handled In terms of notification, severance, out-placement services, etc.?

10-5

Are there formal metrics in place for measuring and rewarding performance over time?

10-6

How effectively has the company communicated its top three business goals?

10-7

I am a hard worker. I expect to be around other hard-working people. Am I going to be comfortable with the level of effort I find here?

10-8

Is the company's training strategy linked to the company's core business objectives?

10-9

How does your firm handle recognition for a job well done?

10-10

When was the last time you rewarded a subordinate for his or her efforts? What token of appreciation did you offer?

10-11

How does the firm recognize and learn from a brave attempt that didn't turn out quite as expected?

10-12

How much freedom would I have in determining my objectives and deadlines?

10-13

How long has this position existed in the organization? Has its scope changed recently?

CHAPTER 12

12-1
Is there anything personally or professionally that you believe would prevent my being a solid contributor in this role?

12-2
Mr. Employer, your search is over. You will not find anyone else more qualified to do this job than I. If I were you, I'd cancel all the other interviews and make me an offer.

12-3
Mr. Employer, I'm not going to keep it a secret. I really want this job, and I know I will be fantastic in it.

12-4
Until I hear from you again, what particular aspects of the job and this interview should I be considering?

12-5
I know I can meet the demands of the position and would make an outstanding contribution. Can I have the offer?

12-6
What will be your recommendation to the hiring committee?

12-7
I'm ready to make a decision based on the information I have. Is there anything else you need to make me an offer?

12-8
I am very interested in this job, and I know your endorsement is key to my receiving an offer. May I have your endorsement?

12-9
It sounds to me as if we have a great fit here. What do you think?

12-10
It has been an interesting and fruitful discussion. I would very much like to take it to the next step.

CHAPTER 13

13-1
What's the gross profit margin of the division I will be working in? What percentage of the total profit from the company does it generate? Is it increasing or decreasing?

13-2
What's your company's "killer application"? What percentage of the market share does it have? Will I be working on it?

13-3
Can you give me some examples of the best and worst aspects of the company's culture?

13-4
What makes this company a great place to work? What outside evidence (rankings or awards) do you have to prove this is a great place to work? What is the company going to do in the next year to make it better?

13-5
What would I see if I stood outside the front door at five o'clock? Would everyone be smiling? Staying late or leaving early? Would everyone be taking work home?

13-6
Lots of your competitors have great products and people programs. What is the deciding factor that makes this opportunity superior? Are you willing to make me some specific "promises" on what you will do to make this a great experience for me if I accept the position?

13-7
Can you show me that the company has a diverse workforce and that it is tolerant of individual differences? Does it have affinity groups or similar programs that I might find beneficial? Is there a dress code? Can you give me an example of any "outrageous conduct" this firm tolerates that the competitors would not?

13-8

Does your company offer any wow! benefits? Does it pay for advanced degrees? Dos It offer paid sabbaticals? On-site child care? Relocation packages? Mentor programs? How are these superior to those of your competitors? What about job sharing? Flex-time arrangements? Telecommuting? Workout facilities?

13-9

When top performers leave the company, why do they leave and where do they usually go?

13-10

When was the last significant layoff? What criteria were used to select those to stay? What packages were offered to those who were let go?

13-11

Does the company have a program to significantly reward individuals who develop patents/great products? Is there a program to help individuals "start" their own firms or subsidiary? Will I be required to fill out noncompete agreements?

13-12

How many approvals would it take (and how long) to get a new $110,000 project idea of mine approved? What percentage of employee-initiated projects in this job were approved last year?

13-13

How many days will it take for you (and the company) to make a hiring decision for this position?

13-14

Who are the "coolest" people on my team? What makes them cool? Can I meet them? Who is the best and worst performer on the team, and what was the difference in their total compensation last year? Sell me on this team and the individuals on it that I get to work with. What makes my closest coworkers fun great people to work with?

13-15

What is your "learning plan" for me for my first six months? What competencies do you propose I will develop that I don't currently have? Which individual in the department can I learn the most from? What can he or she teach me? Can I meet that person? Does the company have a specific program to advance my career?

13-16

Assuming I'm current with my work, how many days could I not show up at the office each week? Could I miss a day without your advance permission? What percentage of the people in this position telecommute? Has anyone in the group been allowed to take a month off (unpaid) to fulfill a personal interest?

13-17

Give me some examples of the decisions I could make in this job without any approvals. Can you show me the degree of autonomy and control I will have in this position?

13-18

How many hours a week do you expect the average person on your team to work? How many hours does the average person in fact work? Are there work-life programs in place to promote a healthy work-life balance?

13-19

How will my performance be evaluated? What are the top criteria you use? What percentage of my compensation is based on my performance? Is there a process where the employees get to assess their supervisor? If I do a great/bad job in the first 90 days, how, specifically, will you let me know? What are the steps you would take to help me improve? How do you discipline team members?

13-20

What is the first assignment you intend to give me? Where does that assignment rank on the departmental priorities? What makes this assignment a great opportunity?

13-21

How many hours of your time can I expect to get each week for the first six months on the job? How often will we have scheduled meetings?

13-22

If I were frustrated about my job, what specific steps would you take to help me overcome that frustration? How about if you were frustrated with me? Can you show me examples of what you have done for others in your group in the past year to overcome any frustration?

13-23

What are the wows! of this job? What are the worst parts? And what will you do to maximize the former and minimize the latter? If I asked the incumbent what stinks about the job, what would he or she say? Can I talk to him or her?

13-24

What will make my physical work environment a fun and stimulating place to spend time?

13-25

What inputs do employees get in departmental decisions? In hiring and assessing coworkers?

13-26

Could I get a chance to see the team in action? Can I sit in on a team meeting? Shadow someone for a day?

13-27

What are the biggest problems facing this department in the next six months and in one year? What key competencies have you identified that I will need to develop in the next six months to be successful?

13-28

What do you see in me? What are my strongest assets and possible weaknesses? Do you have any concerns that I need to clear up in order to be the top candidate? What is the likelihood, in percent terms, that you will make me an offer?

13-29
What is the best/toughest question I could ask you to find out about the worst aspects of this job? How would you answer it? If you were my best friend, what would you tell me about this job that we haven't already discussed?

MEMORABLY
GOOD QUESTIONS

1. What's the makeup of the team as far as experience? Am I going to be a mentor, or will I be mentored?

2. What does this company value the most, and how do you think my work for you will further these values?

3. What kinds of processes are in place to help me work collaboratively?

4. What attracted you to this company, and what do you think are its strengths and weaknesses?

5. Can we schedule a performance review in three months?

6. What are the most critical factors for success in your segment of the business?

7. What can I bring Company XYZ to round out the team?

8. In what area could your team use a little polishing?

9. Do team members typically eat lunch together, or do they typically eat at their workstation?

10. What's the most important thing I can do to help within the first 90 days of my employment?

11. My research shows that Company XYZ is your most aggressive competitor. Is that your judgment as well, and what steps are you taking to differentiate yourself?

12. Do you have any questions or concerns about my ability to perform this job?

13. When top performers leave the company, why do they leave and where do they usually go?

14. What was the last fun thing that you did that wasn't work-related?

15. What do you see in me? What are my strongest assets and possible weaknesses? Do you have any concerns that I need to clear up in order to be the top candidate?

16. You know, this position sounds like it's something I'd really like to do. Is there a fit here?

17. I think I'm good for the job. I really want the job. How can we work it out?

18. Who are the "coolest" people on my team? What makes them cool? Can I meet them?

MEMORABLY
BAD QUESTIONS

1. Can I switch jobs with the hiring manager?

2. Does the company provide snacks?

3. Will they fire me for not wearing any underwear? My last boss was very upset when he found out, and I want to get the issue out of the way early.

4. I need to leave the interview for a minute. Do you have a match?

5. What would you do if the coffeepot were empty?

6. If I don't take a lunch break, can I accumulate the time that I am forgoing and add it to my vacation time?

7. So what is it exactly that you guys do?

8. Are there any apartment complexes nearby that offer a fitness center and free wine and cheese tasting?

9. Why do I have to fill out this job application? It's all on my résumé.

10. What's the story with the receptionist?

11. What is the policy on long-term disability.

12. What's your policy on dating coworkers?

13. Have you been playing pocket pool?

14. May I work on Christmas Day?

15. Before you tell me about your benefits, can I go get my wife? She's in the car and she's the one who wants to know about the benefits.

16. I have custody of my niece and can get child care only three days a week. Can I bring her to work with me the other days?

17. I don't have any experience, so can I get a job in management?

18. What do you pay me if you fire me?

19. I just want to get rich and then get out. How long will that take?

20. If I work here, would I get an office or a cubicle? I'd really like to be able to close the door.

21. How long it is going to be, exactly, before I get a job from your company?

INDEX

Integrated Design, Inc., 14, 41–42
Interaction with others, 23
International Business Machines
    Corporation (IBM), 51
Internet sites for research, 41–46
Interruption of interviewer, 11–13
Interview, purpose of, 6, 103–104
Interviewer
    agreement with, 13–14
    inappropriate questions about,
        32–33, 96
    interruption of, 11–13
    last question by, 1
    note-taking, 50–51
Interviewer, alienation of
    candidate's personal habits, 1–2,
        64, 65, 66
    coworkers, questions about, 77,
        92
    deal-killing questions, 33–34
    humor, 28–31
    inducing defensive attitude,
        14–17, 133
    note-taking, 50
    personal questions, 32–33, 96
    risky candidate, 69–70, 77
Interviewer, candidate relationship
    with
    hiring manager, 81–84
    human resources personnel,
        69–79
    inclusive language, 14
    post-rejection, 158–159
    rapport, 7, 28–31, 129
    recruiters, 59–68
    strategy tailored for, 57–58
    trust, 56, 68
Irrelevant questions, 22
IT (information technology),
    111–113

J
Job description, 5–6, 109–111
Job offer
    asking for, 20–22, 40, 88, 103,
        127–137
    disclosing other offers, 18–19,
        136–137
    hiring authority, 36–38, 57–58,
        81–102
    post-reception, 147–151
    rejection, 153–159
Johnson, Bob, 118
Jones, Kathi, 5

K
Kador, John, 15
Kale, Wayne, 119
Kathnelson, Richard, 6, 73, 121
Keuka College, 9
Killer question, 10
KnowledgePoint, 51, 55, 131, 157
Koch, Ed, 30, 123

L
Landry, Houston, 60
Lane Powell Spears Lubersky, 130
Last question by interviewer, 1
Leading questions, 17–18
Length of questions, 11
Levine, Nancy, 29–30, 132
Litigation, fear of
    feedback during interview, 123
    rejection, 155
    risky candidate, 69–70, 77
Loaded questions, 17–18
Long Island University, 71

M
Magill Associates, Inc., 71
Management Recruiters, 50

About the Author

John Kador is an independent business writer, journalist, and the author of a number of books about careers and the Internet. His most recent career books are *Internet Jobs: A Complete Guide to the Hottest Jobs on the Net* and *The Manager's Book of Questions: 751 Great Interview Questions for Hiring the Best Person,* both published by McGraw-Hill. He is also the coauthor, with Amir Hartman and John Sifonis, of *Net Ready: Strategies for Success in the E-conomy.*

Based in Geneva, Illinois, Kador writes for a number of business publications such as *Electronics Business, Infoworld,* and many others. He received an M.S. degree in public relations from the American University and a B.A. in English from Duke University. More information about Kador may be obtained from his Web site, www.jkador.com. He welcomes questions from readers at jkador@jkador.com.